UP AGAINST IT
by
JAMES PHILIP

CHRISTIAN FOCUS PUBLICATIONS

Published By
Christian Focus Publications Ltd
Geanies House, Fearn IV20 1TW
Ross-shire, Scotland, UK

The substance of the contents was given as a series of sermons in Hollyrood Abbey, Edinburgh.
The spoken form has been largely retained.

Printed in Great Britain

CONTENTS

Dedicated to
my son
William
a great encourager

Cover picture courtesy of
Highlands and Islands Enterprise.
Cover design by Seoris N. McGillivray.

1

INTRODUCTION

The subject of the series of studies which form the substance of this book is one which represents a growing pastoral problem in our day - the incidence of spiritual depression, that experience of despondency reflected in the Psalmist's words, "O my God, my soul is cast down within me" (Ps 42:6).

We look at this subject not merely for the benefit of those who are at present cast down in various ways, but also in a more general way for the benefit of all; for when we are able to grasp firm and clear principles in this matter, it may well be possible to forestall, by anticipation, at least some of the attacks from which none of us are wholly immune. It is always true that, in a time of need, a mind well stocked with the teaching of the Word and with biblical principles is in an immeasurably superior position to one that is not.

First of all, we need to set the parameters of our study, and give some indication of what will and will not be dealt with. It is necessary to limit our enquiry in this way because of some pitfalls which it will be wise to avoid if at all possible. One of these relates to the present-day 'in' theme of counselling. Everybody seems to be jumping on this bandwagon; and if it is asked 'What is wrong with that?' the answer must be that it can lead to an uncritical adoption of principles and practices that may be open to serious question. It is possible, for example, to become preoccupied, if not obsessed, by counselling 'techniques' and become 'sold' on psychological jargon, and to interpret the gospel in psychological terms.

This can prove a very expensive error. A shrewd and penetrating critique made more than thirty years ago by the then President of the Union of American Hebrew Congregations on the subject of what he called 'American Religiosity' seems still strangely up-to-date and relevant to our present-day situation in Britain. He said:

God is made to serve, or rather to subserve man, to subserve his every purpose and enterprise whether it be economic prosperity, free enterprise, security, or peace of mind. God thus becomes an omnipotent servant, a universal bell-hop, to cater to man's every caprice; faith becomes a sure-fire device to get what we petulantly and peevishly crave. This reduction of God from master to slave has reached its height, or rather its depth, of blasphemy in the cult of the Man Upstairs - the friendly neighbour-god who dwells in the apartment just above. Call on him any time - especially if you are feeling blue. He does not get the least bit upset with your faults and failings and, as for your sins, not only does he not remember them... but the very word and concept of sin have been abolished and 'adjustment' or 'non-adjustment' have taken their place.

It can hardly be denied that this is a fair and penetrating criticism of the thinking and attitude among evangelicals today. This is evidenced in the proliferation of counselling or therapy groups that 'go overboard' in amateur psychology and psychiatry techniques. In this connection we would be wise to heed Alexander Pope's admonition in the words,

A little learning is a dang'rous thing;
Drink deep, or taste not the Pierian spring;
There shallow draughts intoxicate the brain.

There is a real danger in 'playing the psychologist or psychiatrist' with flimsy apparatus. We should really leave this to the experts.

Another pitfall lies in the confusion between 'spiritual depression' (as expressed in the Psalmist's words 'My soul is cast down within me') and what may be called 'clinical depression'. What we need to learn is that spiritual ministry cannot well cure medical conditions, any more than medical treatment can cure spiritual problems. While it is of course true that there can often be a combination of both the spiritual and the medical in a condition of depression, it is nevertheless necessary to be able to distinguish between the two, and to discern things that are different in this whole area.

There are several issues here: one is a historical one.

There was a time when the vogue was to explain all human behaviour in psychological terms. For example, if a man did something wrong his wrongdoing tended to be excused on the ground that it was traceable to some trauma in his childhood - and thereby responsibility for it was evaded. It became the fashion almost to blame everything on things that had happened when you were three-and-a-half years old. This went to absurd extremes in some quarters, in which all emotional and psychologocal problems were explained and explained away in this manner.

Predictably - and inevitably - a reaction set in against this foolish extravagance, and in some places the opposite extreme took over; all emotional, psychological and even mental disorders were now attributed to moral and spiritual root causes. The line now was: deal with the spiritual issue, the question of guilt, and this will solve the problem. There is no such thing as mental illness, it is at root a spiritual problem. This in turn has also gone to such extremes in some quarters that it makes a nonsense of the whole issue.

Both extremes are in fact wrong. And if the former does despite to the critical issue of moral responsibility, the latter fails to recognise the reality of organic mental illness that causes deep clinical depression. Untold harm, too can surely be done by supposing that that kind of condition can be solved by dealing with it as a spiritual problem involving guilt. There is a great need here to be able to distinguish a medical condition from a spiritual one.

Another consideration could be mentioned at this point. It can hardly be denied that there is a good deal of ingrained suspicion of psychiatry as a branch of medicine on the part of a great many Christian people. Because of this, they are often simply not prepared to have any dealings with it unless they can be sure of seeing a Christian psychiatrist. One can well understand such a suspicion; but where a medical condition is involved, what we need is not so much a Christian psychiatrist as a competent one. If I have a duodenal ulcer which requires surgery, what I would want is not so much a Christian surgeon as a competent one, one who was good at his job. Similarly, if I am suffering from clinical depression my need is not so much a Christian psychiatrist as a skilled and competent one.

But medical or clinical depression is not really the subject of this book, for a minister of the gospel is not a psychiatrist, and he should not try to be one. This is not his discipline, and his skills lie in a different direction, namely in the exposition, interpretation and application of Scripture, and in the exercise of pastoral care and counsel in the light of that Scripture; that is to say, in areas of experience in which spiritual rather than medical problems arise.

There is in fact a great deal in the Scriptures on this subject, not only in the Psalter but also in other parts of both the Old and New Testaments; and it is worth reminding ourselves that such spiritual giants as the Apostle Paul passed through frequent times of pressure and difficulty. He writes, for example, in 2 Corinthians 1: 8 ff.

For we would not, brethren, have you ignorant of our trouble which came to us in Asia, that we were pressed out of measure, above strength, insomuch that we despaired even of life: But we had the sentence of death in ourselves, that we should not trust in ourselves, but in God which raiseth the dead:

Who delivered us from so great a death, and doth deliver: in whom we trust that he will yet deliver us.

There are those who would say, "When you are a dedicated Christian, that will not happen to you." They feel that Christians should not have such problems, and that it is a measure of their failure as Christians if they do. Are we then to say that Paul was a failure, that he was out of joint spiritually at this point? Who would dare to say such a thing? This is a very cruel, as well as a simplistic, way of thinking, which does not fit the facts of the situation. One of the objectives of this book is to see that some of the giants of the faith suffered in precisely the way that we sometimes suffer, under the pressures of life.

We may take David as a case in point. In Psalms 42 and 43 he is clearly in a state of deep despondency; and in other Psalms we see him in a similar condition, albeit for different reasons and with different causes, such as when things were wrong in his life.

There is also the well known story of Elijah under the juniper tree, in 1 Kings 19, crying in utter dejection "Now let me die."

In the New Testament we see John the Baptist, that mighty prophet, depressed with dark doubts (Luke 7; 19 ff). He was in prison, of course, and it was understandable that a cloud should have come upon him, constraining him to send his disciples to Jesus with the question, "Art thou he that should come, or look we for another?" There is an immense wistfulness and questioning in these words. He was, in fact, in a depressed condition. We see doubting Thomas, in the disciple band, with his gloomy, almost fatalistic, attitude to life: "Let us go to

10

Jerusalem and die with him". Thomas was the sort of person who could always see a dark side in any situation, even if the sun was shining brightly; he was a natural pessimist. We see Timothy, beset with fears and low-spiritedness, longing to escape from difficult situations.

All these are different expressions of despondency of spirit, and we shall look at them as such in the course of our studies, to see what we can learn from them, and whether we can see ourselves in them, and find the help they found.

The Psalmist says in Psalm 42, "Why art thou cast down, O my soul, and why art thou disquieted in me?" There are several different answers that can be given to this question, for the problem of depression or despondency can have all sorts of different causes. It is important, therefore, in seeking to give real help, to ascertain the cause of any particular manifestation of it. Proper diagnosis is always a necessary preliminary to an effective cure.

It is true, of course, as we have already suggested, that sometimes the reason for being cast down lies in sin and failure; and we need hardly look beyond the Psalter for evidence of this. There were times in David's experience when his consciousness of being cast down was certainly due to the fact that he had done wrong, and sinned, and that he needed to be restored to fellowship with God. The Apostle Peter is another case in point: he was in a deep gloom and darkness during the period between Christ's death and resurrection because he had denied his Lord. This, however, applies to unbelievers just as much as to believers, for it is possible for either to be out-of-joint with him. A guilty conscience - by this we do not simply mean a sense of guilt, for one can have a guilty conscience without having a sense of guilt at all - can induce depression, and sometimes the only way out of it is a genuine evangelical experience of conversion, and of entering into peace with God. That is one clear and simple aspect of the problem.

Unconfessed sin can also lead a believer into the depths. We may recall how David, in the wonderful 32nd Psalm, after extolling the blessedness of the man whose transgression is forgiven, goes on to say,

When I kept silence, my bones waxed old through my roaring all the day long. For day and night thy hand was heavy upon me... I acknowledged my sin unto thee, and mine iniquity have I not hid. I said, I will confess my transgressions unto the Lord; and thou forgavest the iniquity of my sin.

When he kept silence, when he did not confess, when things were not right between him and the Lord, it was like something festering within him, bringing him into a condition of deep depression.

Something else may be said on this particular aspect of the subject: it is possible for a believer to be in a depressed state not because God has not forgiven his sin, but because he has not yet forgiven himself. Sometimes one of the hardest things in the Christian life is to accept God's forgiveness and, on the basis of that, to forgive oneself. There are some people who never forgive themselves for what they have done, even though God has forgiven them; and this will certainly lead to depression.

Sometimes, however, depression can be caused by the very ordinary factors of overstrain, overwork and exhaustion. This was surely the cause of Elijah's dejection under his juniper tree. He had been involved in the tremendous confrontation with the prophets of Baal on Mount Carmel, then he ran all the way to Jezreel. That, as we say, was the straw that broke the camel's back, and a very deep reaction set in. Such a condition, caused or precipitated by physical, mental and emotional exhaustion, can sometimes be very devastating. The interaction of bodily strain and mental and emotional pressure upon the spirit can be such as to bring about an exhaustion that issues in deep depression.

Depression can, of course, also be caused by the opposite of overstrain, by inactivity, when people do not have enough to do. The housewife, for example, who has had for years the burden and responsibility - and the fulfilment - of running the home and looking after the family may face this possibility when the children grow up and leave home, and she is left in the home, with her husband out at work all day. She has nothing to do, and becoming bored she may also become depressed. Similarly, the businessman coming to retirement, if he has not made adequate plans for the development of new interests, may well begin to feel he has nothing much left to live for, and lapse into a deep despondency and gloom of spirit that could become critical. It is certainly not by accident that pre-retirement conferences have become a prominent part of the social scene today.

Depression can also be caused through having a wrong orientation to life. When one is basically discontented with one's lot, or refusing to accept it; when one is refusing to come to terms with oneself; when one fails to recognise basic facts about human life - all these are potential danger-spots and potential causes of very real depression. When you get someone who spends the most of life trying to be someone he was never meant to be, or - worse still - pretending to be someone he was never meant to be, sooner or later that person is going to meet big trouble in terms of depression, because he is wrongly orientated to life. He has not come to terms with himself; and this is an important and indispensable necessity for true living.

Then, there are problems related to temperament, and this is a very fruitful area where we can misunderstand ourselves and others. Some people are extrovert, they are breezy, cheery, outgoing, always on the bounce, while others are basically introvert, quieter, more reflective, and introspective. Now recognition here is important, if only to enable us to take steps to counteract extremes, in either direction. If we have introspective tendencies we have to put a brake on these, and recognise that too much introspection can be dangerous. It is true, of course, that we are told in the Scriptures to examine ourselves, and there has to be this close scrutiny of heart and spirit; but some people are always poring over their inward state to see what is going on. This is morbid, and can assuredly lead to depression. We must take steps therefore to prevent it.

We have also to recognise that God works along the line of temperament, and saves along the line of temperament. That is to say, one's basic ground work of temperament remains. We should not misunderstand this. God can, of course, transform human life, but he does not change an introvert into an extrovert: that is not what redemption is about. What happens when an introvert is saved is that he is saved from an unhealthiness in his introversion, amongst other things. But he remains an introvert - not in the bad sense, but simply in the sense that this is basic truth about his character and temperament. Because this is so, a believer should not be discouraged or feel inferior or a failure if he does not become, in his experience of salvation, like someone else who has a very different temperament from himself. And he must beware of trying to induce this. To 'know thyself' in this respect is very important.

If this were understood and appreciated more, it might save young Christians particularly from all sorts of pitfalls. Let us suppose, for example, that a breezy, cheery extrovert has been converted, and that he gives a testimony in public. It is predictable what his testimony will be: it will follow an extrovertish line. And those who listen will say, "What a wonderful testimony!" And so it is, and we praise God for it. But if there is an introverted Christian listening to it, unless he knows himself and knows these things, he is going to say, "Oh dear, my experience is not a bit like that!" and he will begin to lash himself, he will begin to drive himself, he will begin to try to be what God never meant him to be. He will begin to try to induce this cheery, breezy, extrovertish kind of behaviour, and all that will happen is that he will turn himself into a kind of spiritual freak, because this is not what God wants him to be! God wants him to be himself, not someone else. We must not force ourselves into an alien mould. It is when we do that a great deal of trouble starts.

There is another all-important consideration: behind and beyond all these factors we have mentioned, there is the fact of Satan. In this connection two things can be said: on the one hand, the enemy of souls can take any or all of these, and give them a subtle twist, doing untold harm to a human life. On the other hand, he can sometimes bring a direct attack upon the human spirit. It would almost seem as if this was the explanation of Paul's experience in 2 Corinthians 1:8ff.; it was not that the Apostle was wrongly orientated to life, or under strain through exhaustion (although doubtless he was often in such a position) but that the evil one made a frontal attack upon his soul. But this aspect of the subject will occupy us more fully in a later chapter.

One other thing that requires to be said is this: we need to bear in mind the condition of society today. It is fair comment to say that there are far more stresses and strains and pressures in society now than there were even twenty or thirty years ago. Since this is so, I do not really think that it helps very much when the older generation says, as it is sometimes prone to say, "This did not happen in our day, you should pull yourself together." This is not a very helpful attitude, although one can see the force of it, and in some situations it is the very word that people need. But life prior to 1939 and the Second World War was in fact much more stable than life is today, and the tremendous pressures that surround younger people and younger families now were just not known in the pre-war years. This is undoubtedly a factor in all our considerations of the subject of depression. I say this merely to fill in the picture, and to show that we are dealing with a very complex and complicated problem; and since this is a very complex and complicated problem we must beware of any glib, and facile, and even simplistic, attitude. It does not help simply to say, "Take it to the Lord in prayer." There are times when an attitude like this can verge on the blasphemous, and this is not the attitude that we are seeking to adopt. Our concern is to be biblical, and to understand some of the things that the Scriptures say to us on this subject.

The message of Psalm 73 is a case in point. Here is a man conscious of the pressures upon his spirit, and feeling himself floundering, losing all footholds, as in agony of spirit he wrestles with his perplexity, doubting the goodness and the fairness of God. "When I thought to know this, it was too painful for me; until I went into the sanctuary of God; then understood I...." (vv.16,17). Such is the way in which the Psalmist found an answer to his perplexities; and this is where we must find ours. But this is where a major problem lies, because when we are under pressure what tends to go by the board are things like going to the sanctuary, reading the Scriptures, saying our prayers. It is very difficult to continue reading the Scriptures or to pray when our spirits are low, for the heavens seem as brass, and the instinct of our hearts is to give up. This is where 'maintaining the motions' is such an immensely important and essential thing to do. We must keep at it. "Hope thou in God," says the Psalmist elsewhere (42 :11), "for I shall yet praise him, who is the health of my countenance, and my God." This is our purpose in the studies that follow.

2

THE HORROR OF GREAT DARKNESS

Genesis 15:12: "And when the sun was going down, a deep sleep fell upon Abram; and, lo, an horror of great darkness fell upon him."

After a long but necessary preamble and introduction to the subject of spiritual depression we are now ready to examine the teaching of Scripture itself. And we begin with the experience of Abraham. I refer you to the significant statement in Genesis 15:12 which speaks of Abraham passing through a dark night of the soul. I ask you to consider with me that profoundly moving phrase "a horror of great darkness fell upon him." In a strange kind of way there is an encouragement for us lesser mortals in the fact that such a spiritual giant as Abraham should have known and experienced such a darkness as this. It is a measure of how we sometimes misunderstand and misinterpret the Bible that we should suppose that the saints mentioned in the Scriptures were supermen, and not people like ourselves. The truth of the matter is that the best of God's servants pass this way from time to time. One of the great comforts to me in my early days of ministry was to learn from the reading of Christian biography how many of the greatly used men of God in the history of the Christian Church had times of darkness and melancholy just like this, and would certainly empathise with this remarkable phrase.

Let me be personal for a moment or two in this regard. While I was meditating on this subject I suddenly recalled a summer evening many years ago when, in loneliness and utter distraction, I walked the shore and rocks where I lived, feeling as if my spirit would be quite overwhelmed by the sheer weight of the heaviness that was upon me at that time. I walked these rocks like a man demented. Tennyson's words,

> Break. break, break,
> On thy cold gray stones, O Sea!
> And I would that my tongue could utter
> The Thoughts that arise in me,

and,

> Tears, idle tears, I know not what they mean,
> Tears from the depth of some divine despair
> Rise in the heart, and gather to the eyes,

reflected my mood as I paced the shore in utter distraction and near despair. To mention this will perhaps explain why Spurgeon's *Lectures to My Students,* and especially the chapter entitled 'The Minister's Fainting Fits,' has meant so much to me over the years (this is a book that should be prescribed reading for all servants of God, not only ministers, but all who seek to serve him in the gospel). In one passage Spurgeon instances Martin Luther as a case in point (and it is surely a comfort to know that even he was no stranger to the dark night of the soul), and says,

> The life of Luther might suffice to give a thousand instances, and he was by no means of the weaker sort. His great spirit was often in the seventh heaven of exultation, and as frequently on the borders of despair. His very deathbed was not free from tempests, and he sobbed himself into his last sleep like a great wearied child.

And that was the mighty giant of the Reformation!

Professor Emil Brunner, in a chapter in his *Dogmatics* entitled 'Angels and the Devil,' says,

> It is precisely those Christians who have the deepest Christian experience who have the greatest personal experience of the reality of the power of darkness.

and he then quotes words from a poem about Luther,

> His soul is the battlefield of two worlds,
> I marvel not that he sees demons.

It will be observed that this is giving a reason for Luther's experience of darkness, namely, that it was in relation to his calling and to the strategic work that God had given him to do. The same can certainly be said about Abraham, and indeed about many of the other giants of the faith. Spurgeon himself, that remarkable man who towered over the spiritual life of London for more than forty years in the nineteenth century, exercising a unique ministry of powerful utterance in the gospel, says,

> Knowing by most painful experience what deep depression of spirit means, being visited therewith at seasons by no means few or far between, I thought it might be consolatory to some of my brethren if I gave my thoughts thereon, that younger men might not fancy that some strange thing had happened to them when they became for a season possessed by melancholy; and that sadder men might know that one upon whom the sun has shone right joyously did not always walk in the light.

That was certainly the case with the mighty Abraham.

I invite you, then, to examine Abraham's story in this light, to seek reasons for this dark and terrifying experience. I wonder if you have ever noticed how lonely Abraham's life was. True, he had people round about him, his wife, his nephew, and all his retinue; but the impression nevertheless persists as we read through Genesis that he was isolated by his calling to be the father of the faithful. There is almost a monolithic quality about his aloneness; and I think that is a constituent part of every man's calling to the work of God, particularly in the ministry. I well recall being deeply impressed when I first read a poem by the French poet, Alfred de Vigny, on Moses, the man of God. In a remarkable and very beautiful poem there is a recurrent refrain as Moses expostulates with God.

> Am I to live always then powerful and solitary?
> O let me sleep the sleep of the tomb.

That is a very perceptive insight into Moses' life and experience, because he also was a lonely man, and there must have been times when he, like Elijah, had the longing to be relieved of the burden. That is surely one factor in this situation of the dark night of the soul. There are times when the sense of isolation and of aloneness sweeps upon one with overwhelming force. Spurgeon says, in telling words:

No one knows, but he who has endured it, the solitude of a soul which has outstripped its fellows in zeal for the Lord of hosts. It dares not reveal itself, lest men count it mad; it cannot conceal itself, for a fire burns within its bones: only before the Lord does it find rest.

Such a solitude was certainly one factor in Abraham's experience that contributed to the 'horror of great darkness' that fell upon him.

Another is this: we need to bear in mind the antecedents of this dark experience that led up to it. In the previous chapter of Genesis we read of Abraham'a campaign against, and victory over, the heathen kings who had held Lot his nephew captive. It is a remarkable chapter, full of thrill and excitement, but we cannot doubt but that it took a great deal out of Abraham. And then, in chapter 15, we read, "After these things, the word of the Lord came unto Abram in a vision saying, Fear not, Abram." The question that arises is why this should appear at this particular point in the record? What was the cause of his fear? The enemies had been defeated. God does not have to say, 'Fear not', to fearless men. What we have to recognise is the sense of reaction that Abraham experienced after the strain of battle. It is usually after some great exploit that the danger point arises. In time of crisis one usually finds resources to bear one through, but it is after the crisis is over that the reaction sets in. This is one of the things that the Apostle Paul had in mind in his tremendous utterance about the Christian armour in Ephesians 6:10 ff., "Take unto you the whole armour of God, that ye may be able to withstand in the evil day, and having done all, to stand." That is to say, it is after the evil day is over that it is important to be still standing, without crumbling.

That is where Abraham is here, after the great exploits of chapter 14; and that is the critical point when we can be assailed and cast down.

One readily thinks of Elijah's experience on Mount Carmel (1 Kings 18), where he was absolutely magnificent in his challenge to the prophets of Baal, standing there like a giant, fearlessly facing them. But the next chapter tells of Jezebel's threats against him, threats which on any other occasion he would have brushed off with contempt, but which on this particular occasion proved to be the straw that broke the camel's back, and he suddenly crumpled, and fled in disarray to the wilderness, and wept like a little child under the juniper tree, wailing out his pain and grief and sorrow to God, "Now, Lord, let me die, for I am no better than my fathers." Reaction was the cause of Elijah's collapse, and that is one factor which we see in this chapter.

And if we recognise this, we are in a position to take some preventative action so that we do not fall in this way. This is one of the lessons that we need to learn.

Also, we need to consider what the encounter with Melchizedek, the mysterious priest/king, must have meant to Abraham, and done to him. We are told that "Melchizedek brought forth bread and wine.... and blessed" the patriarch. We need to read between the lines in this interview, for it was clearly a deep spiritual experience.

Melchizedek in effect said to him, "Abraham, I see that you have a great future in the purposes of God, greater and vaster than anything you could imagine. Great and wonderful things are ahead of you." We can hardly doubt that a sense of awe and high responsibility came upon the patriarch in that encounter, in the consciousness of the unknown that lay ahead of him. What would we feel if a mysterious personage came to us and pronounced such a verdict on our life, that God had a purpose for our life bright beyond all our imagining? Would we not be inclined to say, like Paul, "Who is sufficient for these things?" Here is the loneliness of being a 'front-runner', so to speak, in the purposes of God, and the sense that we are trapped, shut up, into faith. Would it be misunderstood, if it was said that there is a terrible ruthlessness about God when he lays his hand upon a life, not ruthless in the sense of arbitrary cruelty, God forbid, but ruthlessness in the sense of the irrevocable solemnity of being shut up unto the purpose of God? That was a factor in this horror of great darkness that came upon Abraham.

But there was also something else: there was the matter of the promise that God had given him. This is what lies behind what Abraham says in Genesis 15:2: "Lord God, what wilt thou give me, seeing I go childless?" The promise that had been spoken of earlier was as yet unfulfilled. This is one of the things that can lead to the horror of great darkness. God had spoken, but nothing seemed to be happening. "Can I be mistaken?" thinks Abraham? "Is it all an idle dream?" God had said, "Look now towards heaven, and tell the stars if thou be able to number them." And he said unto him, "So shall thy seed be." Abraham had believed God and it was counted to him for righteousness. And it was after this that the horror of great darkness came upon him.

It is impressive to trace a similar pattern in the experience of others in Scripture, and it should encourage us in our own times of darkness to realise that they may be very closely related to future blessing in our lives.

It was when our Lord had received his anointing at Jordan that he was driven straightway into the wilderness to be tempted of the devil. It was on the borders of the Promised Land, on his return from Laban's household, that Jacob wrestled with the angel. It was on the threshold of his life's work that Moses had that strange and terrible encounter with God (Exodus 4:24). These things are written for our learning and encouragement. God does not always let the sun shine on us, for we must learn to walk by faith, in the darkness.

But there is another consideration also. The sense of the unknownness of the future may well, in particular circumstances, bring a gloom and depression upon the spirit. As one commentator has put it,

> God's promise, so far from making everything in the future easy and bright, is that which above all else discloses how stern a reality life is; how severe and thorough that discipline must be which makes us capable of achieving God's purposes with us. A horror of great darkness may well fall upon the man who enters into covenant with God, who binds himself to that Being whom no pain nor sacrifice can turn aside from the pursuance of aims once approved.

Viewed in this light, the darkness becomes understandable. Calvin, commenting on this passage, has this to say:

> It is, however, to be observed, that before one son is given to Abram, he hears that his seed shall be, for a long time, in captivity and slavery. For thus does the Lord deal with his own people; he always makes a beginning from death, so that by quickening the dead, he the more abundantly manifests his power.

The horror of great darkness, then, is a kind of death, with all its attendant pain and suffering, grief and mystery, and yet it is out of this that God's grace and power emerge. As such it has a deep symbolic significance, as the verses which follow serve to explain - a foretaste, so to speak, an emblem, of what Abraham's seed was to pass through ere the promise of the covenant was fulfilled to them - a kind of prophetic preview of his dealings with them. As to Israel, his natural seed, it signified the bondage in Egypt before they reached the promised land; as to Christ, the promised Seed, it surely signified the Cross that was to be endured for the joy that was set before him; as to believers, as Abraham's spiritual seed, it signifies that we must through much tribulation enter into the kingdom of God.

When we pass through a dark night of the soul, therefore, we must consider that it may be in relation not merely to past experience, but to what is yet to come in our lives. I could not know, when I paced the seashore in distraction these many years ago, that just around the corner, so to speak, God had purposes to bring me to Edinburgh to exercise a ministry here. But in retrospect I could not doubt that the loneliness, agonies and pains - and failures too - of these early days were a training ground, preparing me for what I was yet to do. And I know that I could not have done what I have been enabled to do, had it not been for these earlier years of preparation. We need to stand back and see life in some kind of divine perspective.

Spurgeon in his own inimitable way says, "Before any great achievement, some measure of the same depression is very usual. Surveying the difficulties before us, our hearts sink within us." And he adds,

Such was my experience when I first became a pastor in London. My success appalled me; and the thought of the career which it seemed to open up, so far from elating me, cast me into the lowest depth, out of which I uttered my miserere and found no room for a gloria in excelsis. Who was I that I should continue to lead so great a multitude? I would betake me to my village obscurity, or emigrate to America, and find a solitary nest in the backwoods, where I might be sufficient for the things which would be demanded of me. It was just then that the curtain was rising upon my life-work, and I dreaded what it might reveal. I hope I was not faithless, but I was timorous and filled with a sense of my own unfitness. I dreaded the work which a gracious providence had prepared for me. I felt myself a mere child, and trembled as I heard the voice which said, 'Arise, and thresh the mountains, and make them as chaff.' This depression comes over me whenever the Lord is preparing a larger blessing for my ministry; the cloud is black before it breaks, and overshadows before it yields its deluge of mercy.

There is an 'afterwards', then, in the gracious purposes and providences of the living God. Abraham found it to be so, and so, surely, shall we, in the experiences through which we pass. And this should serve to assure our hearts, when the darkness comes upon us. Nor must we forget the safeguarding element in God's dealings with us. Spurgeon is right when he says,

Men cannot bear unalloyed happiness; even good men are not yet fit to have 'their brows with laurel and with myrtle bound', without enduring secret humiliation to keep them in their proper place. Whirled from off our feet by a revival, carried aloft by popularity, exalted by success in soul-winning, we should be as the chaff which the wind driveth away, were it not that the gracious discipline of mercy breaks the ships of our vain glory with a strong east wind, and casts us shipwrecked, naked and forlorn, upon the Rock of Ages.

Here, then, is Abraham, a spiritual giant, the father of the faithful, passing through an experience described as a horror of great darkness coming upon him, not because he is lacking in faith, not because he is failing in some major issue, but solely in relation to the purposes of grace that God had for his life. And what we need to recognise is the significance of the marvellous verse in Exodus 20:21, spoken of Moses but equally applicable to Abraham: "Moses drew near unto the thick darkness *where God was*." If that is the truth of the matter, it does not matter how dark it becomes: God is there. The trouble is that we do not always or often have that consciousness when we are passing through such an experience, because it is of the essence of the darkness that we feel alone and forsaken, even by God. If we were always sure that God was in the darkness it would be comfort and reassurance to us. This is one of the functions of Scripture, to assure us that it is so.

This is the Word of God. This is what he says about the dark night of the soul. He is in the thick darkness and he speaks to us in it, as he spoke to Abraham. Indeed, he spoke to such purpose that the patriarch was given a preview of the history that was to befall his seed, when as yet he did not even have a son let alone a progeny. And what follows in the subsequent chapters of Genesis tells of the fulfilment - progressive, unhesitating, inexorable - of the sovereign purposes of God for his life. But he had to enter into that horror of great darkness in order to learn this. It was something abundantly worth learning. A realisation of the truth of this will bring light into our darkness also, and give us an understanding of God's dealings of grace and love with his children.

3

"GUILT IS MY SHADOW"

Genesis 32:24: "And Jacob was left alone...."

We turn now to another Old Testament figure, again from the book of Genesis, Jacob, the grandson of Abraham. And here is a very different kind of situation, and a different kind of pressure upon a man. Often, in studying the story of Jacob, what is brought out is the stark and often shattering challenge that the story affords us of a man who was far from what he should have been for so many years despite having been the recipient of the grace of the covenant. We look at it now, however, from a different viewpoint, to see the light it can cast upon why God's people are sometimes hard-pressed with spiritual darkness or depression; and - more importantly - we need to see the grace and love of God present throughout the story, breaking in again and again and again to help and to encourage, and also to heal. Indeed, this is really the point of our studies: to show how hard-pressed people can be pointed to the God of all grace and help.

We consider first of all - briefly at this point, and then in more detail presently - the pattern of Jacob's experience in the light of our present theme of spiritual depression. There is Jacob's experience that led up to the marvellous Bethel manifestation in Genesis 28. It does not need much imagination surely to realise that this was one of the darkest hours of Jacob's life. Then there were the long years of exile recorded in Genesis 29-31 in his Uncle Laban's homestead, years that were turbulent and darksome, with many bleak passages of frustration, disappointment and conflict. Then there was Peniel, in Genesis 32, when Jacob was left alone, and the angel of God came and wrestled with him in an awesome and indeed terrifying experience of crisis. Then there were the darker years of Jacob's middle and later life (which are often forgotten about), when the clouds came on, bringing grief and desolation to his spirit through family dissension and family problems, and the feeling that everything had gone wrong and was against him.

I hope it will be seen what was meant by saying that God's grace and love were reaching out to him all the way through, at Bethel during the dark years when the angels of God met him, at Peniel when his name was changed from Jacob to Israel, and even in the years of sorrow and heartbreak, in his old age, when he was able to speak of "the angel that redeemed me from all evil" (Gen.48:16). The picture we are given is of a God seeking to break in, eager indeed to succour, to help, to redeem - even, and perhaps especially, at the times when there seemed to be no thought or consciousness of God in Jacob's mind and experience at all. Though it is very impressive to see from Genesis 29-31 how little mention of God there is in Jacob's ongoing turbulent experience, almost as if he were in the background and had been relegated (as indeed he had been) by Jacob himself, yet God's presence was so truly there, working silently for him.

Something should be said at this point about the traditional interpretation put upon Jacob's story. It is often held that Bethel represents a conversion experience for Jacob, and that Peniel indicates a more decisive experience in which he was really changed into a new man. This is an over-simplistic picture, which does not happen to fit the facts of the situation. There is ample evidence of continuing tension and crisis in Jacob's experience that went on right to the end of his days; and it could just be that the writer to the Hebrews had this in view when he wrote, "By faith Jacob, when he was a dying, blessed both the sons of Joseph..." That, to him, seems to have been the salient point of Jacob's story - not Bethel, not Peniel, but when he was a-dying, as if to suggest that it took all that time for things to be resolved in the patriarch's life, and for him to enter his true destiny.

The point that needs to be underlined is this: all along there seem to have been unresolved problems and issues in Jacob's life, and therefore there were continuing crises and tensions. These could be described, for want of a better word, as depressive episodes, and they continued because he continued to be out of joint with God. Perhaps the truth about him is that he did not have very much self-perception as to the nature of his own problems, and was therefore unable to grasp in any adequate way the significance of God's dealings with him.

This provides a useful key to an understanding of the things that happened to him. One thinks, for example, in relation to the Bethel experience, of the circumstances leading up to that crisis point. There is the sorry and sordid tale of family disloyalty within his home, with his mother Rebecca aiding and abetting her wily son to filch from his brother Esau the birthright and the blessing, and the horrible deception at her instigation practised upon the aged Isaac. It was entirely predictable that Esau should have vowed vengeance upon Jacob, forcing him to flee his home, with his mother's falsely reassuring words ringing in his ears, "Arise, flee thou to Laban my brother to Haran and tarry with him a few days...."(Gen.27:43 ff), days that were destined to stretch into twenty long years, before he saw his home again.

It does not need much imagination to visualise Jacob getting as far as Bethel and feeling that he had already had enough. Having fled the murderous fury of his brother, he was now far from home, footsore and weary, lonely and cast-down, and smarting under a sense of guilt. He did not know what the future would hold, and was conscious perhaps most of all that it was his sin that had led him into such an impasse.

One thinks of many of the Psalms which record David's distress and gloom, and his consciousness that it was things that he himself had done that had brought his darkness upon him. Something of this is surely echoed in the Bethel story, when after the marvellous vision of the angels of God ascending and descending the ladder, Jacob cried "How dreadful is this place...." Why should this have been his reaction? It was that religion, having been a traditional family concern, but having never really touched his life in any deep sense, suddenly, for the first time became a reality for him, as he encountered a real and living God. Suddenly, he was very, very afraid, with a fear that betokened that he was out of joint spiritually. This must surely bear some relation to the conflict with feelings and emotions in his heart and spirit at that time, in his realisation that it was the things that were wrong in his life that were the cause of all his trouble.

Further on in the story, in the record of the turbulent years he spent in the household of Laban, it is impressive and significant to see how Jacob was tricked and beguiled by the wily Laban just as he had tricked and beguiled his own brother Esau, and how his hopes in the love affair with Rachel were frustrated and dashed. Such an experience must certainly have proved extremely painful and heartbreaking to him. One wonders whether he ever thought to relate the distresses that he experienced to the things that he had done to others. At all events, the chapters which record his sojourn with Laban provide us with the biography of a man for whom many things seem to have gone wrong, and who was permitted to reap the shame and sorrow of his self-chosen way. The truth is that, notwithstanding his experience of grace at Bethel, he was still a man intent on taking matters into his own hands, a scheming opportunist, often having recourse to unworthy and sinful expedients to gain his ends, as he had been before he left home. There had been so little change in him over the years, and so little self-perception about the nature of his problem. So much needed to be done in his life that it is little wonder that God kept him in Haran for so long.

The record of Jacob's encounter with the angel at Peniel constitutes another landmark in his experience. Genesis 32 is a remarkable chapter, encapsulating in itself several distinct emphases which reflect Jacob's complex and complicated nature and temperament. For one thing, we see him preoccupied with his forthcoming meeting with his brother Esau after so long a time. We are told that he was 'greatly afraid and distressed', and these words bear witness to the power of a guilty conscience. His apprehension was surely related to the approach of Esau, whom he had wronged twenty years previously. But something else is evident also. We are told at the beginning of the chapter that the angels of God met him on the way. It was as if God were saying to him, "If only you will trust me, Jacob, and let me order the course of events, all will yet be well." But Jacob was apparently constitutionally incapable of trusting simply in God, and once more we see his agile, scheming mind at work, planning and making arrangements for every possible eventuality with such resourceful cunning that we want to cry out in exasperation, "Oh Jacob, stop, stop, stop! Have you forgotten the assurance that the presence of the angels of God gave you on the way?" Even his wonderful prayer, recorded in the earlier part of the chapter, which by itself must stand for all time as a model of true prayer, as he cast himself upon the covenant mercy and grace of God, seems to lose its point when it is followed by the same old scheming opportunism as before. If he had really believed, would he not have known the rest of faith in his heart that would have kept him from his feverish precautions?

Whatever else might be said about Peniel, this much has to be said, that it represents the past catching up with Jacob. His preoccupation may have been with the forthcoming meeting with Esau, but a more fateful meeting was destined to take place. Jacob was left alone. Sometimes, in the economy of God, this is engineered for us, because it is when we are utterly alone, and all our defences are down, that God can get to us. Against the background, and in the context, of his twenty years' discipline in the wilderness, discipline which had failed to bring him to a place of real trust in God, we begin to understand that God lost patience with this schemer, and took a grip of him, that left a permanent mark on his life, and something was broken in him for good. God wants our willing surrender to his will and purposes, but when after long patience it is slow in forthcoming, he sometimes has to touch our natural powers and resources, and touch them permanently, reducing us to impotence before we learn the needed lessons. Jacob's wrestling seems to stand as a symbol of his whole life - he always resisted the Spirit and it was this that led to the drastic action at Peniel. It was a costly day, but fruitful; judgment and mercy met in that fateful hour, and Jacob went limping into the sunrise.

There is a sense in which the whole issue of Jacob's life and experience is summed up in the question the angel asked at Peniel, "What is thy name?" Twenty years earlier, in the sordid episode of the stolen blessing, Isaac had asked him a similar question, "Who art thou?" And Jacob answered, "I am Esau." This was the lie that had characterised his whole experience and had become 'second nature' to him. It was now exposed, as the angel obliged him to recognise himself as he really was. This was the cause of all the turbulance and the upheaval in his life, the rocky road he trod with its frustrations, darkness and gloom.

Frances Thompson's poem 'The Hound of Heaven' ends with the penetrating words:

> Is my gloom, after all,
> Shade of His hand, outstretched caressingly?

How much this says about Jacob's experience! Jacob was crippled by his encounter with the angel. But it is better to be crippled by God than crippled by sin.

It still remains true, however, that long after this tremendous encounter we still see Jacob with unresolved problems and difficulties in his life, and one is prompted to conclude that there remained with him a disturbing lack of self-perception that continued to make life more difficult for him than it need have been. If his story has anything to say to us, it surely constitutes a plea for self-awareness - not a morbid probing of our inmost hearts, but a self-awareness concerning the things that condition our attitudes day by day, that make our lives spiky, awkward and difficult. For this is a necessary prerequisite in any process that leads to wholeness of life.

4

MAKING THE LOAD LIGHTER

Exodus 18:18: "This thing is too heavy for thee; thou art not able to perform it thyself alone."

For our next study we turn to the patriarch Moses, and to an important and significant incident in his experience, recorded in Exodus 18.

In our study on Abraham's experience of 'the horror of great darkness', reference was made to a remarkable poem by the French poet Alfred de Vigny, in which he spoke of the loneliness of Moses:

> Je vivrai donc toujours puissant et solitaire?
> Laissez-moi m'endormir du sommeil de la terre.

> Am I to live always, then, powerful and solitary?
> Let me sleep the sleep of the earth (tomb).

We pointed out that this is often one major factor in the situation of depression. There are times when the sense of isolation and aloneness sweeps upon us with overwhelming force. And we quoted Spurgeon's words:

No one knows, but he who has endured it, the solitude of a soul which has outstripped its fellows in zeal for the Lord of hosts: it dares not reveal itself, lest men count it mad; it cannot conceal itself, for a fire burns in its bones; only before the Lord does it find rest.

Moses surely knew something of this in his experience, and there are hints of it in the chapter now before us. What we read here, however, comes under the heading of prevention rather than cure. As such, it has a great deal to say to us.

The language of some of these verses as translated in the N.I.V. is very graphic:

Moses' father-in-law replied, 'What you are doing is not good. You and these people who come to you will only wear yourselves out. The work is too heavy for you: you cannot handle it alone. (v. 17)
....the simple cases they can decide themselves. That will make your load lighter, because they will share it with you. If you do this, and God so commands, you will be able to stand the strain... (v. 22)

Impressive words, indeed, and compelling; and we might well take the phrase 'making the load lighter' as our title here, so accurately does it describe the message of the chapter.

By way of introduction, however, something needs to be said about another kind of interpretation of this passage that has sometimes held the field. The construction placed upon this episode by the footnotes in the Scofield Bible is that 'Jehovah entirely ignored this worldly-wise organisation, substituting his own order' (cf Numb. ll:l4-l7). But this is an interpretation which must be disputed as having no real foundation in fact. Indeed, Jethro's words to Moses, quoted above, have a 'right ring' about them, and the more we contemplate and study them, the more we see their wisdom and their application. It is not too much to say that the adoption of this advice and counsel given to Moses saved him from serious burn-out and breakdown. That is the value of the story for us.

The godly and saintly expositor Dr. F.B. Meyer, in following the line of interpretation which a plain and straightforward understanding of the text seems to require, draws attention to a noteworthy parallel to this incident found in Acts 6:1 ff.. In a situation similar to that of Moses, the Apostles delegated authority to men of ability, of good report, full of the Spirit and of wisdom, whom they appointed to look after the administration of the daily distribution to the widows of the fellowship, on their behalf. Meyer adds, "In each case the increased organisation was a sign of vitality, and led to the immediate strengthening and increase of the entire movement." We know, from Acts, that after the appointment of these deacons, there was an accession of power in the early Church and its fellowship. Let us study the situation in some detail, and learn some lessons from it.

The Tyndale commentary says, of Jethro's words in v.l4, "Why sittest thou thyself alone....?", that they are "the wise question of an old chieftain who has learned the great lesson of how to devolve authority. Like many a Christian leader, Moses was wearing himself out unnecessarily (verse 18) by trying to do everything single-handed. This is not always a mark of ambition; it is sometimes the mark of the over-conscientious and over-anxious. More, it was wearing out the people (verse 18 again), an aspect usually overlooked."

This is a very telling point, and there is ample evidence all around to indicate that this is something that happens frequently. It happens in business, in industry, in the professions, and not by any means least in Christian work and service. Men and women drive themselves into the ground, hurting not only themselves, but also those around them, whether associates or their families. This is what Jethro had seen in Moses' situation, causing him deep concern and prompting his wise counsel.

One recalls what was once said to another giant of a man, in the later history of the Old Testament: "Arise and eat; because the journey is too great for thee" (1 Kings 19:7). God had to minister to a man who had been 'going it alone' for too long.

Jethro saw what was happening, and it was this that prompted him to intervene. We should bear in mind that he was a priest who ministered to the living God (v.12). We should not lightly dismiss him as a heathen priest, since there are significant hints in the Old Testament record that there were men outwith the covenant who were in fact men of God. Melchizedek was one such, a priest of the Most High God, and it may well be that Jethro was another. At all events, he saw the immense, and indeed insupportable burdens that Moses was bearing, and he said to himself, "This is an impossible situation; the man will kill himself if he does not watch out. He is wearing himself out. I must say something to him, to try to make his load lighter."

There is a great deal in this story that we must seek to investigate, first of all, in relation to the personal dynamics that lead to such a situation of over-stress; second, in relation to the prescription held out by Jethro; and finally, in relation to the complex and complicating factors which sometimes make it very difficult to accept such counsel and put it into practice.

We look first of all, then, at the personal dynamics involved in such a situation. The Tyndale commentary, quoted above, gives one hint: sometimes the driving force may be a question of personal ambition, the determination to be better or more successful than anyone else, whether as a business man, an industrialist, a church worker or a minister. This is an occupational hazard in many areas of life, and it bids us ask some very pointed questions of ourselves with regard to motivation. We need to ask, "Is my busyness, my over-burdenedness, nothing more than the expression of an inflated ego trip?" Among the vows taken by a Church of Scotland Minister is included the question, "Are not zeal for the glory of God, love to the Lord Jesus Christ, and a desire for the salvation of men, so far as you know your own heart, your great motives and chief inducements to enter into the office of the Holy Ministry?" Zeal for the glory of God or, would it be truer to say, zeal for self-expression or self-aggrandizement? A spiritual zeal or a psychological drive that eats a man up, driving him restlessly and relentlessly into the ground? A question that we often need to ask ourselves is, "What are you trying to prove to yourself?" That is a good question, and its answer is not always obvious, as our next consideration serves to indicate.

Sometimes the problem lies in "the need to be

needed" which often lies at the heart of one's own experience and serves to explain a great deal about our behaviour and attitudes. For this can be an enormous driving force, causing great stress and pressure, since it is an attitude which inevitably ends up by becoming subject to the law of diminishing returns. Those who are the recipients - one might almost say the victims! - of this attitude often finally feel that they have had enough, and this can precipitate great crises in such people when they realise that they are in fact no longer needed.

C.S. Lewis, in his book *The Four Loves,* has created a notable character, Mrs Fidget, who embodies the 'need to be needed' syndrome in her own family situation. Lewis' writing is a piece of very amusing caricature, of course, but it embodies a deeply serious description of an all too common condition, in which a kind of emotional blackmail can operate with dire consequences for all involved, and not least for Mrs Fidget herself. For these deep-seated, and for the most part unconscious, motives constitute a recipe for eventual breakdown, burn-out, cracking up, and even the shipwreck of our faith, and sometimes the acquirement of weakness and illness which people feel they need, in order to retain the attention and care of others, the 'they-cannot-cast-me-off-when-I'm-in-such-need' syndrome - emotional blackmail indeed!

Sometimes over-conscientiousness can be combined with - and indeed be in part explained by - a relentless super-ego, that drives a man beyond reasonable bounds, so that he becomes a workaholic, developing a pattern that he cannot give up. But sometimes it is not nearly so complicated as that, and is little more than the simple overload and over burden of work: "Moses, you are doing too much, you are doing beyond what is reasonable."

The personal dynamics of the situation, that lead to a condition of overstress, are of great, even critical importance, and must be examined with considerable care and sympathetic understanding, if help is to be given.

In the second place, we now consider the prescription held out by Jethro as a solution to Moses' problem. In effect, he said, "You cannot handle it alone. Share it. That will make your load lighter, and that way you will be able to stand the strain." There are several things to note here. There is such a thing as strain in life. Pressure is a fact of life, and no one is exempt from it or can opt out of it. True, some people's threshold of endurance is much lower than others' - this also is a fact of life - and one must learn to accept such people and be tolerant of them and charitable to them. But the great thing is the sharing of burdens.

This is true both in the realm of administration, in Christian work or in business, and also in the common concerns of life - the cares, the toils, the sorrows and lonelinesses, the disappointments and the tragedies - all that may constitute pressure points, and bring the stresses and strains that make life intolerable and not worth living. And this is God's word for such situations: "Share it. That will make your load lighter, and you will be able to stand the strain."

This is the incomparable value of Christian fellowship for the Christian Church is the only place on earth where we should be able to expect to find a caring attitude and a helping hand, and even a listening ear, which is sometimes all that is needed. To be able to tell out our burden to a willing and sympathetic ear, and to find relief in the telling - that is an aspect of Christian fellowship.

This leads to our third consideration, the complex and complicating factors that sometimes make it very difficult to accept such counsel, for there is that in us which almost instinctively makes us want to 'go it alone', and to brood in seclusion on our distress. But the Scriptures frown on such an attitude, in the emphasis they make on the importance of fellowship. The Apostle Paul's words in the great prayer in Ephesians 3:14ff., remind us that we best know and comprehend the love of Christ in fellowship "with all saints". There are blessings in the Christian life that God does not vouchsafe, and that are denied, to the individual believer, but which are bestowed upon the fellowship of saints. This is emphasised in more than one place, and in more than one connection in the New Testament. In 2 Timothy 2:22 Paul exhorts his young colleague to "Flee also youthful lusts: but follow righteousness, faith, charity, peace, *with them that call on the Lord* out of a pure heart." William Still of Aberdeen makes a shrewd and illuminating comment on these words:

Since youth is more actively gregarious than maturer persons, the solution to the impulsive life is to be found in perusing the Christian virtues in fellowship. Yet the tendency of so many excellent young people, sensitive almost to the point of maladjustment, is to 'go it alone', as if the chief human good was to be found in isolation. That this is not so can be proved by an insular young person taking stock of their introspective thoughts when they brood, mope and moon alone: they are largely, if not entirely, social thoughts, of the ideal person or persons they would like to have fellowship with. This needs to be pointed out to youth, that it may know that the way to health, as also to moral stability and Christian usefulness, is the way of fellowship. We are made to be together, and all who are in Christ will be together unto all eternity. No isolation there. Why, then, should we think that any solution of our problems can be found in withdrawing and withdrawnness? We are social beings (albeit it is alone we may learn who and what we are to be in society), and the solution to our problems is to be found in pursuing the fundamental Christian virtues in company with those who are known to be calling upon God out of a pure heart. This cannot be overstressed."

Is not the danger of 'aloneness' the tendency to become self-preoccupied? Overmuch brooding about one's problems, and indeed overmuch praying about them, can be dangerous since this keeps them in the forefront of one's mind, when the greatest need is simply to forget them for a while. Fellowship with others is a necessary corrective, if for no other reason than that we come to realise that there are other problems in the world than our own. Sharing common aims - and burdens - with others, looking forward together, takes our minds off the crushing burden of aloneness and overstrain. 'Going it alone', for whatever reason, is laying upon our system a stress it was really never designed to bear.

In the story of the woman with the issue of blood whom Jesus healed, we are told that when the miracle took place (upon touching the hem of his garment) she would have stolen away quietly, without speaking to anyone. It was Jesus who called her back, and out, into the open, into fellowship and sharing. This was surely a necessary exercise, not in the sense that if it had not so happened the issue of blood might have returned, but rather that all the accompaniments of her condition - the loneliness and isolation and the bleak despair it had brought to her - also required to be dealt with. There is surely a parable for us in this lovely story. And it says this to us: it is in the fellowship that sharing burdens brings that these burdens become bearable, and that we are saved from becoming engulfed in intolerable pressures and despair.

Do we discern in this a word from God for our present need? Have we, when under pressure, felt that it is a mark of weakness to share it, and that we ought to be able to cope with it on our own? Is God saying to us, "What you are doing is not good. You will only wear yourself out. The work is too heavy for you; you cannot handle it alone. Share it. That will make your load lighter." This is his word to the burdened and the overwrought, to lead them into peace.

5

BITTERNESS OF SOUL

Ruth 1:20,21: "Call me not Naomi, call me Mara for the Almighty hath dealt very bitterly with me."

The story of the experience of Naomi, the mother-in-law of Ruth the Moabitess, is one which, in the very distressing circumstances that overtook her, affords some very valuable insights into our theme of Spiritual Depression, especially when we relate its message, as we shall ultimately do, to what is said in Psalms 42,43: "Hope thou in God: for I shall yet praise him, who is the health of my countenance and my God."

One is conscious of a certain reticence in dealing with this story, because of the sensitive nature of the material which it contains, for Naomi was a mourning widow, and in many Christian fellowships there are those who mourn like her, and one would not wish to add in any way to their distress and pain by any ill-considered word or attitude. Our prayer should be that the Spirit of God will overshadow and hallow our study in his own uniquely gracious way, so that hearts that are desolate through bereavement may not be hurt or grieved.

The Book of Ruth unfolds a marvellous and

beautiful story, and it is all the more remarkable to find such a jewel from the time of the Judges, one of the darkest and most sombre periods in Israel's history. It is perhaps not without significance that a time of famine is mentioned at the outset of the story - an evidence that the hand of God was heavy on the land for its sins, and that Elimelech and his family were refugees from Bethlehem because of the famine. The circumstances of that family were therefore imbedded in the ongoing experience of the people of Israel in a time of great moral and spiritual declension, and it may well be that something of this sense of the Divine hand upon the nation rubbed off on Naomi more than she might have realised.

There is an important truth in this. When the smile of God is upon a people, and the Divine grace is bringing streams of refreshing, it is certainly true that individuals enter into and find a share in the national refreshment and renewal. One thinks of the aftermath of the great revival of 1859, when all sorts of blessings came upon all sorts of people, following the outpouring of the Spirit in such fulness. Many of the great philanthropic movements of the later nineteenth century were the result and fruit of the revival - Barnardos, Quarrier's Homes, the Salvation Army, the C.S.S.M., the abolition of slavery - and so many were blessed and enriched by the spiritual upsurge in the life of the Church. In the same way, but in contrast, and conversely, when the hand of God is heavy upon a national situation, individuals may also share in the general gloom that that brings. One thinks, for example, of ministers serving in hard places, with the heartbreak of an unresponsive and indifferent people. This is part of the general judgment that many think lies upon our land at this time.

There is little doubt that Naomi was one who had suffered greatly and deeply, and nothing that may be said about her in this study can alter or minimise that fact. She was bereaved of her husband while they lived in Moab in their self-appointed exile, fairly early, it would seem, in their sojourn there. And ten years later her two sons, who had in the meanwhile married Moabite wives, also died. Her cup of sorrow was surely very full as she felt the desolation and isolation of an Israelite widowhood in a foreign land. This triple misfortune of family tragedy and sorrow must call forth a deep compassion and sympathy in us. All who have known bereavement will appreciate the depth and the bleakness of her grief and desolation. That is not in question; and all that could be said in terms of loving sympathy and compassion must surely be said on her behalf. For sorrow is common to us all, and will knock at every door, soon or late.

The important thing, however - seeing that none of us can hope to have a life without pressure or distress at some times - is what we do with it, and how we relate to it, and cope with it. Naomi's sorrow and grief are one thing; but her attitude to it is another, as may be seen from a consideration of some of the statements she makes in the first chapter of the Book of Ruth. In 1:6, the point at which she made to return to Bethlehem and her own land, we read, "She had heard in the country of Moab how that the Lord had visited his people in giving them bread." The implication, one suspects, is that she was thinking in her heart, "Well, the Lord has certainly not visited me in this way. They are fortunate. I am afflicted." In 1:13, she says, "It grieveth me much for your sakes that the hand of the Lord has gone out against me." We begin to see how her mind was working. The Lord has visited Bethlehem, but he has afflicted her. Is not this an implied reproach of God for what has happened to her?

This seems to come right out into open expression in what she says to her compatriots on her return to Bethlehem:

Call me not Naomi, call me Mara: for the Almighty hath dealt very bitterly with me. I went out full, and the Lord hath brought me home again empty: why then call ye me Naomi, seeing the Lord hath testified against me, and the Almighty hath afflicted me?

There is a remarkable phrase in one of the Psalms (105:18) about Joseph which seems to be very apposite in relation to Naomi's attitude. The circumstances that form the subject matter of the Psalm are similar - the Lord had called for a famine upon the land (105:16); Joseph was afflicted, and the Psalmist says of him, "Whose feet they hurt with fetters; he was laid in iron; until the time that his word came: the word of the Lord tried him." Spurgeon makes reference, in his comments on this Psalm, to the phrase we sometimes use, when we say of a man that "the iron entered into his soul," and suggests that this may be one interpretation of the phrase "he was laid in iron." This is certainly how it seems to have been with Naomi. She was very sore in her sorrow and grief, and alas, very taken up and pre-occupied with it.

One wonders whether there was an element of Rachel's sorrow in Naomi's attitude. What we mean is this: Matthew, quoting from Jeremiah 31:15 ff., says,

In Rama was there a voice heard, lamentation, and weeping, and great mourning, Rachel weeping for her children, and would not be comforted, because they are not" (Matt. 2:18).

The Authorised Version rendering of Jeremiah's words, reads that Rachel *"refused* to be comforted for her children." From which we may learn that, not grief and sorrow, but preoccupation with it, assumes the character of an expensive indulgence that we cannot really afford. Not the grief itself, but over-absorption with it - this is the problem in Naomi's experience.

This prompts the reflection that so often in life - not merely in sorrow and grief but in a wide variety of experience - there are two ways of looking at things. When the patriarch Jacob, in his advancing years, was faced with the pressures of a complicated family situation, he exclaimed "All these things are against me" (Gen. 42:36); but when the apostle Paul spoke of the tribulation of Christian experience, he was enabled to say, "In all these things we are more than conquerers" (Rom. 8:37).

The point that needs to be made is that Naomi's situation could well be looked at in another and different light, in terms of the more positive things she had going for her. In the first place, we may look at the daughter-in-law that God had given her in Ruth, and savour something of her quality. Could there ever be anything more moving, more beautiful, more reassuring, than the words Ruth spoke to her mother-in-law?

Intreat me not to leave thee, or to return from following after thee: for whither thou goest, I will go; and where thou lodgest, I will lodge: thy people shall be my people, and thy God my God: Where thou diest, will I die, and there will I be buried: the Lord do so to me, and more also, if ought but death part thee and me. (1: 16,17)

We may well feel that Naomi could have added another sentence to her statement in 1:21 "......the Almighty hath afflicted me; but look at the treasure he has also given me in this dear girl, whose presence and support mean more to me than I can ever say." But she did not say this. Indeed it does not seem to have been even in her thoughts, or that Ruth's words had even touched her. On her return to Bethlehem, all that was in her consciousness was her all-consuming sorrow and woe.

The lesson is well summed up in the words of P.T. Forsyth:

It is a greater thing to pray for pain's conversion than for its removal... It is not always easy for the sufferer, if he remains clear-eyed, to see that it is God's will. It may have been caused by an evil mind, or a light fool, or some stupid greed. But now it is there, a certain treatment of it is God's will: and that is to capture and exploit it for him.

And Forsyth goes on to say:

Our soul may put on its Sunday clothes, and square its shoulders, and face the world with courage and resolution.

In the second place, we need to recognize the silent working of providence on behalf of this sad and disconsolate lady. We are told in 2:3 that Ruth happened to light on a part of the field belonging to Boaz, who was of the kindred of Elimelech, Naomi's late husband. How wonderfully providence began to work for them both! Boaz had heard of Ruth's devotion to the stricken Naomi (2:11,12). He was aware of the nature of Ruth's help, although Naomi was too preoccupied to appreciate it. And that divine providence was silently planning in love for both of them, had she but known it, for an issue brighter than she conceived at the time. And the wonderful love affair that followed is one of the priceless gems of all literature. God was at work in the situation, and it is not too much to speak of the smile of tenderness and boundless compassion on his face as he looked upon Naomi in the bitterness of her grief and her refusal to be comforted, as if to say, "I am going to do things for her that will turn her mourning into joy."

In the third place, there was something even greater going for Naomi - something infinitely greater - which becomes clear in the last chapter of the story. The genealogy recorded in the final verses of the book is full of significance, indeed it is not too much to say that the whole purpose of the book having been written is enshrined in the unfolding of this line of promise. For the geneology traces Boaz's ancestry from Pharez, the son of Judah, the son of Jacob and in turn unfolds his progeny down to King David. Ruth was thus incorporated into the royal line of promise, which brought forth in the fulness of the time David's greater Son, the Lord Jesus. In a remarkable and wonderful way, therefore, the sovereign, redemptive purposes of God for the world were in operation in the sorrow, grief and desolation of Naomi.

We may well make reference once again to the words in Jeremiah 31:15 ff., about Rachel's weeping and refusing to be comforted, for the prophet goes on to say,

> Thus saith the Lord; Refrain thy voice from weeping, and thine eyes from tears: for thy work shall be rewarded, saith the Lord; and they shall come again from the land of the enemy. And there is hope in thine end, saith the Lord.

There is hope in thine end - God was saying to her, "This will have a gracious issue." Here was a grief-stricken widow, whose world had come apart, and who felt that life was never going to be the same again - but she was wrong, so wrong. When the God of grace is involved, sorrow and tragedy never have the last word in the human story.

All of which brings us to the message unfolded in Psalm 42, for this is a Psalm which tells us what we may do to counteract the bitterness that Naomi's experience displays, and how to prevent the iron from entering into our souls, in their refusal to be comforted.

The picture in the opening verses of the Psalm is a moving one. The scholars tell us that the Psalmist is probably living in exile, and compelled to sojourn far away from Jerusalem and its worship. The reference could well be to the time David fled the city during his son Absalom's rebellion. If so, we may well understand the sense of desolation and the agony of longing in his heart, which he expresses in the beautiful picture of the hart panting after the water brooks. Perhaps he is out in the open, pacing about in distraction of spirit, when he sees the thirsty hind straining to find water; and sees a picture of himself in the incident. At all events, it is not difficult to see in his experience a reflection of many different experiences of darkness and desolation through which we ourselves may pass from time to time.

In his agony of spirit, the Psalmist recalls how it used to be with him. He remembers the old days, how he rejoiced in the worship of God and the fellowship of his people: "I had gone with the multitude, I went with them to the house of God, with the voice of joy and praise, with a multitude that kept holy day" (42:4). And this puts him. as it were, on the horns of a dilemma: for to remember these things is in one sense a comfort, yet in another their remembrance, by comparison with his present distress, makes that distress doubly distressing. Thus his soul pours out in bitter-sweet desire. His anguish and torment of spirit are very deep.

But now, in 42:5 ff., a different note is struck, and we become conscious of a conflict of opposite emotions in which, as Maclaren puts it, "streaks of brightness flash through the gloom," and, "sorrow is shot with brightness." It is almost as if another voice had broken into his pained soliloquy. And in one sense another voice has broken in. The Psalmist tries to take himself in hand. He speaks to himself. He gives himself a talking to. "Why art thou cast down, O my soul? Why art thou disquieted in me? Hope thou in God. for I shall yet praise him for the health of my countenance." An old Puritan writer says, "David chideth David out of the dumps" (Trapp). Here, then, are two Davids, the one who is a victim of these dark and terrible moods of depression, and the other the rational self, that is, the spiritual rational self. The one is summoned to give account of himself to the other: "Why art thou cast down?" And the rational self sets over against the undoubted woes and distresses of the other the great objective facts of divine grace, and says, "Hope thou in God."

This is faith in the dark, indeed: for he does not feel in the least like this, or that he could ever praise God again. But faith asserts itself, and this is always the beginning of victory. Victory does not come yet, of course, at this point, not indeed until some time afterwards; but it is the introduction of a principle, a consideration, which ultimately makes victory certain and inevitable. In this connection it is important to see that it is not somebody else saying this to us: it has to be ourselves saying it to ourselves. So long as it is only someone else saying it, whether preacher, counsellor or friend, the 'feeling' self and the 'rational' self are both inactive and supine, gripped by self-pity and distress. But when 'we' take 'ourselves' in hand, things will begin to happen.

Here, then, is God's word to the Naomis' of this world: Give yourself a talking to, chide yourself out of the dumps, until the dark night of the soul yields to the morning. And with the hymn writer say,

Then, with my waking thoughts
Bright with thy praise,
Out of my stony griefs
Bethel I'll raise,
So by my woes to be
Nearer, my God, to thee,
Nearer to thee!

6

IN THE DEPTHS

1 Kings 19:4: "It is enough; now, O Lord, take away my life."

It would be difficult, in pursuing any study on the theme of spiritual depression, not to turn to a consideration of the experience of the prophet Elijah, as he sat under the juniper tree wanting only to die. This must be the theme of our study now. We have already made reference to Spurgeon's comments on Martin Luther; 'seasons of fearful prostrations' which have been the experience of so many of the most eminent of God's servants: and this is more than a little reflected in the story of Elijah. Like Luther, Elijah was a big man, a giant in the faith, and one who was utterly sure of God, a man who had fearlessly and magnificently challenged King Ahab and the prophets of Baal in the tremendous confrontation on Mount Carmel, taunting and mocking them at the silence of their god and his inability to answer their cries, then calling down the fire of God on the sacrifice. The triumph of light over darkness was complete, as he announced to Ahab that there was the sound of abundance of rain. It was a moment of glory indeed. Such is the message of 1 Kings 18.

But the scene and the atmosphere change equally dramatically at the beginning of 1 Kings 19. Here is a picture of total dejection, and indeed, almost disintegration, with the prophet in a state of total collapse. The picture that we have at this point in the record is so utterly different from all else that we learn about Elijah that we almost wonder if we are reading about the same man. But it is the same man, and in this dramatic change there is a good deal for us to learn.

One question that arises is whether such a change was something completely out of character, or simply the expression of something that was always there in Elijah's temperament, and brought out at this point by a particular combination of circumstances. This is an important consideration in the matter of spiritual depression, for there is such a thing as a temperament that is constitutionally prone to periodic lowness of spirit; and when this is so, one must strive to avoid the kind of circumstances of stress and strain that might tend to precipitate it. There seems little to indicate that Elijah was of such a temperament, and it may well be that it was rather a series of extraordinary pressures, and a combination of them, that brought about Elijah's distress and despair.

It would be much too facile a judgment to suggest that sudden cowardice and craven fear laid hold upon the prophet, making him flee from the wrath of Jezebel. This would entirely fail to do justice to the very complex and complicated factors in the situation, or to recognise that there was something essentially illogical in Elijah's reaction. For Jezebel's threat was not a new one: it had been made before, and voiced repeatedly by

Ahab, as the previous chapters make clear; and the calm courage of the man of God had met it unmoved. But now, on this occasion, something seems to have snapped within him, and he fled. In almost any other circumstances he might have ignored it; but at this point it was the straw that broke the camel's back.

Furthermore, it will hardly do as an explanation to say that what a man really is comes out in a crisis. Can we apply this judgment to Elijah's situation? We must not forget that there were two crises here - one at Mount Carmel, and the other at Jezreel, when Elijah got Jezebel's message. And they brought out totally different reactions in the same man. If, then, we are to say that what a man really is comes out in a crisis, which is the true picture: Elijah on Mount Carmel, magnificent in his opposition, or Elijah under the juniper tree? And which was more dangerous for him? Which would we have preferred? Surely the first crisis on Mount Carmel was infinitely more dangerous for Elijah than the second; and yet in the Mount Carmel situation he showed himself a giant; it was in the latter that he crumpled. This shows the danger of glib and facile theories. To say that what a man is comes out in a time of crisis is a statement which requires to be qualified very substantially in a situation of this nature. The fact is, we see the real man in both the crises: human nature is capable of both heights and depths.

We must bear in mind, therefore, the element of illogicality in depression, and recognise that there is often something in it which defies analysis or explanation. Paradoxically, there is something immensely comforting and reassuring in this. For, moral and spiritual giant though he was, Elijah was also, as James points out in his epistle, "a man of like passions as we are." It is not a little reassuring to realise that such a man could descend to this state and want only to die. Well, God did not let him die. He had other plans for him; indeed, he went up in a chariot of fire, in triumph. It may well be that this is a word of assurance, comfort and hope to some despairing soul, that there will be a blessed end to his dark experience, more glorious than he could dare hope for or even imagine at this stage.

There are a number of things that can be said about Elijah's situation. The first is that he was in a state of severe reaction, following a time of tremendous spiritual and emotional pressure. After great exploits for God, this is a very real danger. In the aftermath of the glorious victory at Mount Carmel he was seriously overwrought - who would not have been? - and a serious reaction set in, bringing a dark and enervating depression upon his spirit. He was 'not himself', and this explains much of what was out of character in his behaviour. We must remember that the life we live is a life lived in the flesh; and even the best of God's servants are subject to its frailties and weaknesses. Becoming believers does not make us supermen.

It has been suggested that where Elijah went wrong was to have run all the way from Carmel to Jezreel, and that this was beyond his strength, and brought on the extreme reaction. Over-reaction, it is said, leads to depression. This is true, but who are we to say that this is how it was with Elijah, or that it could have been avoided? There is no evidence in the text that he did wrong; rather, what we can gather is this: if we are going to do battle with devils, as Elijah did, this may well prove to be part of faithful service and discipleship.

One has only to look into the New Testament to see some of Paul's autobiographical statements in this connection: "In weariness and painfulness..." (2 Cor 11:27). What do we suppose these words mean? They mean that Paul had occasions and experiences in which he was 'not on top of the world' but desperately weary, pained in mind and spirit, and with the sentence of death upon himself, despairing even of life. "You are killing yourself with too much work" - that is what would be said to Elijah today. But whose fault is this? "I only am left." Where were all the others? God said, "There are yet seven thousand who have not bowed the knee to Baal." But where were they? That was what Elijah would be wanting to know!

Here, then is a situation in which crisis has brought reaction, and the prophet is overwrought and brought down into a dark depression of spirit. It is true that we do not have this kind of crisis in respect of battles against the prophets of Baal, but there are things in human experience that can correspond to it in all sorts of ways. There may be a combination of trying circumstances which can build up pressure in such a way that something snaps, and the human spirit is not able to bear it. It is not difficult for us to think in terms of problems and pressures of one kind or another, all of them, it may be, by themselves tiny and insignificant compared with Elijah's pressures on Mount Carmel, but together proving a sizeable problem, and bringing this kind of reaction.

At such times as these some very basic realities must be recognised. For one thing, when depression of this nature grips us we do not see clearly, and we cannot think clearly. Everything is distorted and we are unable to see things as they are. Therefore it is not a time for making decisions or initiating plans, because the chances are that we are going to make the wrong decision or initiate a wrong plan of action. The situation is not in fact all black, for God is still in control. We can see, as Elijah could not, that he was going to live to fight another day, and work for God again, and better than before. But one cannot see that when one is depressed in spirit; and therefore it is extremely unwise to be making decisions either in one's home or in one's family, or about one's job. It is far wiser and safer to maintain the status quo until the time of pressure is past. Christian action must be guided by reason, not by mood. This is where the danger lies. It is in times of depression that we do things, and say things, that we afterwards regret. We must remember the illogicality of the situation, and wait till the shadows flee.

For another thing, we must also remember that this is a situation that the devil delights to take hold of and use mercilessly. Satan can gain an advantage over us in this way, with his black clouds, with his terrifying insinuations and accusations. We may recall how in *Pilgrim's Progress,* Christian was subject to these terrible pressures from the evil one in the Valley of the Shadow. We shall be dealing with this at a later stage, and simply mention it now.

There may, however, have been another reason for Elijah's dejection of spirit. It could well be that there had come to his heart a sudden consciousness that the tremendous battle on Mount Carmel had not been as decisive as he had at first thought. To be sure, Ahab's initial reaction must have been at one with the people's, as they cried, "The Lord, he is the God," as he witnessed the fire of God coming down from heaven; but Jezebel's fury must certainly have given him second thoughts, as she vowed vengeance upon the prophet. And with Jezebel's message there must have come the realisation that Ahab's reaction, which had seemed so promising, proved to be a thing of straw. It is surely not difficult to imagine Elijah's conflicting thoughts as he made his way south to Beersheba. To have held hopes for almost a lifetime - and Elijah was coming towards the end of his ministry - that God would turn the land again to himself, and to have felt that the victory at Carmel was surely the realisation of these hopes, and to see them so cruelly dashed, was too much for him, and he felt he could not take any more.

Alongside this too, there may well have been something even more distressing, a secret disappointment with God, the feeling that he had let him down, that at the critical moment he had not delivered the kingdom, when Elijah thought he should have done, and could have done. This is a very sensitive area: disappointment with God is not something we readily voice. It would be terrible for any man to say, "O God, you are a disappointment to me," but this may well be how his heart is feeling. And when a man gets to that position in the numbness of his distress and dejection, what can he do, and where can he turn? It is surely very understandable that he should say, "It is enough; now, O Lord, take away my life; for I am not better than my fathers."

When we turn to a consideration of how God dealt with his overwrought servant - in abject misery as he was, exhausted physically, mentally, emotionally, spiritually, at the end of his tether and wanting only to die - perhaps the most important thing to say on a superficial level is that God did not utter a single word of rebuke to him (it is Satan who does that to the saints). Rather, he ministered to him very wonderfully as he lay exhausted under the juniper tree, sending an angel who touched him and said "Arise and eat: because the journey is too great for thee" - no reproach, but simply the recognition of Elijah's need, and the Divine provision for that need. There is a lovely, though hidden, significance in this, reminding him of his earlier experience when, in hiding from the wrath of king Ahab, God sent the ravens to feed him and provided the widow to minister to him. It was as if, in producing a cake baked on a fire and a cruse of water, God was saying to him, "Elijah, nothing has changed, you know, I am still God, I am still the One who provides food for the hungry. Remember the ravens, Elijah, remember Zarephath; I am still the same, the unchangeable One." That is a wonderful word to a man who feels that everything has gone to pieces and God seems to have deserted him.

God's prescription in the first instance, then, for Elijah's dejection was sleep, rest and food. In other words, the physical situation was set to rights. This is such an obvious need; but apparently it is by no means obvious to many, who seem to miss it, or fail to appreciate it. It is not a question of probing into the spiritual situation, searching out some spiritual defect, some unconfessed sin that has dried up the life of the Spirit. We know, of course, that unconfessed sin does dry up the life of the Spirit, and that spiritual defects can bring depression of spirit but we must learn that not all depression is caused by sin or by spiritual defect. Very often it is simply something for which overtiredness and overstrain are responsible.

A simple illustration may help here. When one receives a severe blow on the upper arm, the whole arm becomes numb; and depending on the strength of the blow, it may remain numb for some time, until the nerves and tissues recover. In the meantime the numbness means that there is a lack of feeling in one's arm. It is like this, also, with a shock to one's spirit: when one's spirit takes a hammering, a numbness comes, a sense of having been bludgeoned develops, and it sometimes takes a long time to wear off. This is the simple explanation of why some believers in such a situation feel so utterly empty of spiritual feeling. They do not feel the presence of God, there is no joy in prayer, there is no joy in the Scriptures; they are simply numb.

In such an experience, it should be a comfort to realise that it is the prayers of God's people, not our own, that bear us up and along, and that we can rest upon their prayers, without being worried too much that we cannot ourselves pray with any feeling.

Thus, gently and tenderly, then, was Elijah ministered to by the Lord; and, once his physical condition was attended to, one might almost say that the Lord turned his attention to his mental, emotional and psychological need. The experience at Horeb, in the remarkable theophany of the earthquake, wind and fire, must certainly have been a stimulus to his jaded mind. We should not underestimate this very human need, in our assessment of the problem of complete spiritual renewal and restoration. The old adage, 'All work and no play makes Jack a dull boy,' has more basic spiritual insight than we might imagine. To be sure, mental weariness and dullness can be greatly accentuated by an overwrought state, but lack of adequate mental stimulus is just as likely to be responsible for these conditions. It has been noted by one missionary organisation that in the rigorous conditions of the mission field missionaries who did not have some cultural interest tended to crack up far more easily than those who did. This is too significant a fact to be passed over lightly. A spirituality that neglects either mind or body is not truly biblical in its emphasis. God's care is for the whole man, body, mind and spirit, and thus did he minister to Elijah - first his bodily needs, then the mental stimulus afforded by the theophany, and finally the still, small voice speaking to his spirit.

We cannot doubt that there was a deep spiritual challenge to Elijah in the still, small voice that spoke to him, and that God had a purpose in speaking to him in this particular way. There is a sense in which the whole theophany constituted a parable of Elijah's experience. He had indeed been a prophet of turbulence and drama - he had burst on the national scene like a meteor - and his actions at Carmel all partook of the spectacular. But now God was revealing to him that there are other ways by which he speaks. It may be of interest in this connection to recall that on the day of Pentecost the spectacle and drama of the tongues of fire evoked lively interest and curiosity and the question, "What meaneth this?" But it was Peter's sermon, much less dramatic and spectacular, that made them cry out, "Men and brethren, what shall we do?" The still, small voice of God spoke to their consciences in the word of preaching rather than in the mighty rushing wind. It would seem that God was intent upon leading Elijah into deeper things. Still waters run deep, as we say, and this may be the significance of the still, small voice. The quiet persuasiveness of the Spirit avails far more than the force of the spectacular.

This is a lesson we all need to learn, and it is of particular relevance at the present time. There is something in our spirits that craves for excitement, and this can be truly disastrous in spiritual work. "Except ye see signs and wonders, ye will not believe," said Christ, chiding the unbelief of his generation. There are some who are not prepared to wait quietly for God to work, nor to allow him to work quietly and unobtrusively. They must have earthquake, wind and fire, and when God does not oblige, they set about producing them themselves, but the Lord is not in them. As Alexander MacLaren, that prince of preachers, once said, "Souls go away admiring, excited or agitated, but there has been no intercourse with God."

One wonders whether this incident was the answer of God to the secret thoughts of Elijah's heart about the work in which he was engaged. Was Elijah disappointed that God had not accomplished an even more decisive victory over Baal-worship and above all over Jezebel, and was this at least in some measure the cause of his dispiritedness? Was there a desire in Elijah's heart for a once-for-all vindication of righteousness that would establish the kingdom without further delay? And was the parable of the still, small voice an indication to the fiery prophet that God accomplishes his purposes in other, less obtrusive ways?

It is true that Jezebel continued to be a sinister influence for evil in Israel, and that Ahab soon shook off the effects of the great demonstration of Divine power at Carmel; but it is also true that the less obvious, long-term influence of Elijah proved in the end to be far more significant than he could have then realised, for what his ministry did was to create a conscience in the life of Israel to which all his successors in the prophetic office made their appeal with such devastating force in after days. At the end of the day, when the full story is told, that may prove to have been the great and abiding contribution Elijah was enabled to make to the strategic purposes of God in the redemption of the world. But that is much more in affinity with the idea of the still small voice than of the earthquake or the fire.

This should hearten and encourage those who sometimes think they "have laboured in vain and spent their strength for nought" when they do not see a speedy regeneration in the spiritual life of the nation. The fact is, God uses such men at two levels, the obvious and evident one on which men are blessed and victories are won on a limited scale, and also - and this can be seen only after the passing of the years - on the deeper and hidden plane where influence is decisive. Elijah not only routed the prophets of Baal at Carmel, in earthquake, wind and fire; his whole ministry speaking in a still small voice made possible the prophetic ministry for the next three hundred years. That was the real measure of the Divine purposes in and through him.

Two final points may be noted before we leave the story of Elijah. The first is this: the prophet's consciousness of a great loneliness and desolation of spirit expressed in the words "I, even I only, am left" should not and need not be interpreted as merely the evidence of his depressed state at this point in his experience. In times of moral and spiritual declension there is a great loneliness that comes upon the faithful; this is part of the cost of true cross-bearing. Indeed, from the strategic point of view, God cannot afford to have many of his true servants clustered together in one place. Even seven thousand are not many, scattered throughout a population of many millions.

The other point is this: God directed Elijah back into the fellowship of the faithful, back to those seven thousand who had not bowed the knee to Baal. Perhaps Elijah was not very enthusiastic about them; perhaps they did not have the same spiritual insights as he had. But they were God's people, and they could minister to Elijah, and encourage his hand in God. This, in fact, is what did happen on Elijah's return from Beersheba, for the Lord laid his mighty hand upon one of these seven thousand, and called him into training for a life's work of service. It was not only an evidence of God's gracious condescension to his lonely servant in providing him with a companion in his work, in the person of Elisha, a man so much after his own heart; it was also an indication of the unfolding pattern of the Divine strategy for the days that lay ahead.

The ultimate test of any work of ministry is not merely that souls should be gathered into the kingdom of God, but that there should also be those in whose lives the great work of character-building should be manifested, with a view to significant and effective service in the future. A true ministry not only begets enthusiasm for its cause, but also a holy determination, in at least some, to walk in the steps of true discipleship. The tremendous potential of even one such may be seen in the story of Elisha. In the deepest sense, God's Elijahs can never truly say, "I, even I only am left," for they beget like-minded men through their ministry who themselves leave their mark and thereby continue the work that has been begun. All this God's servants should remember in the loneliness of their calling.

7

OUT OF JOINT

Jonah 4:8: "Jonah...said, 'It is better for me to die than to live.' "

There is a sense in which the subject matter of our next chapter, the experience of the prophet Jonah, stands as a companion piece to that of the previous chapter. The common factor is the wish expressed by both Elijah and Jonah that they might die.

It was said, in the study on Elijah, that part at least of the significance of the 'still small voice' which the prophet heard was that he was challenged about his estimate and understanding of God's work and purposes. We suggested that he may have been secretly disappointed with God for not putting a final end to the evil regime in Israel at that time - and was therefore at odds with God. Elijah had to get his ideas sorted out and be shown that God had other ways of working than by earthquake, wind and fire.

The story of Jonah is the story of another man much more seriously at odds with God, and very much out of joint spiritually. In our introductory study we said that having a wrong orientation to life, and failing to come to terms with life, can be a fruitful source of depression. We have a graphic example of this in the story of Jonah, for in it we see how disjointed and out of sorts it is possible for a believer to become, even in the context of the service of God, and indeed of being used by him, as Jonah undoubtedly was.

Briefly, the message is this: there are people who make life very difficult for themselves, more difficult than it need be and more difficult than it should be, because they are at odds with themselves and at odds with God. It can hardly be doubted that this is the explanation of a considerable amount of depression in the experience of Christian people today.

The story of Jonah begins ominously and fatefully. Here is a servant of God, summoned to speak his Word, and he does not want to do it. Indeed, he refuses to do it, and rather than obey he runs away, and takes a ticket on a boat to Tarshish. The story goes on to tell of all that happened to him, and how things go terribly wrong with a man when he gets out of the will of God. Our concern here, however, is not with this part of the story: of how Jonah was in jeopardy of his life, but was nevertheless prepared to lose it rather than do God's will; of how the Lord miraculously preserved him, bringing him to an end of himself, in a profound experience (described in chapter 2), after which he was recommissioned by God and went to Nineveh and preached the message of repentance with dramatic consequences. It is the final chapter of the book that is our concern. There we see the prophet 'back to square one', so to speak, angry once more, and at odds with himself and with God, and - in spite of all that had happened - wanting to die. It is our task to try and understand Jonah's situation, and to see the causes of his dark and distressing mood.

The key to an understanding of Jonah's attitude lies in the opening verses of chapter 4. The end of chapter 3 tells us of the impact Jonah's preaching had upon Nineveh, as a result of which the Lord "repented of the evil that he had said that he would do unto them." His anger was turned away from them. And, as the narrative goes on to tell us, this displeased Jonah exceedingly, and he was angry with God, till the resentment in his heart came pouring out in the extraordinary prayer in 4:2,3. The bitterness of the prophet's outburst against God for showing mercy to the heathen city is an evidence of just how seriously he was out of joint spiritually, and of how partial his repentance and submission to the Divine will had been.

It is, however, possible to misjudge and misunderstand Jonah in this, so far as the underlying reason for such a reaction is concerned. It is clear that behind his attitude there was a fear that God would show mercy to Nineveh. But this was not because he was a hard and bitter bigot, who enjoyed doom-mongering. The real issue was something else: it was his love for his own people, Israel, that made him not want Nineveh to be spared. To say this requires some elucidation, and what it means is well expressed by D.E. Hart-Davies, in his book *Jonah: Prophet and Patriot.*

The prophet, at the first, must have rejoiced greatly at the news that Nineveh was doomed. For if Nineveh were destroyed Israel might be saved. But as Jonah meditated upon the tremendous event, the occurrence of which had been Divinely predicted, and the part assigned to him as the herald of Assyrian overthrow, it began to dawn upon him that there was a possibility, yea, a probability, that the message of warning might prove to be a message of mercy; that, should Nineveh repent, Jehovah might repent and Nineveh be spared! What then must he do? Shall he run the risk? Shall he go to Nineveh and tell the inhabitants thereof that within forty days their city is to be destroyed? He dare not. He is afraid of the Divine compassion. He dreads the tenderness in the heart of God. He is terrified at the possibility of a manifestation of the Divine mercy. So he resolves to disobey. Because he is so pure a patriot he refuses to be any longer a prophet.

Such were the motives that drove Jonah and led him into disobedience - not bigotry, not cowardice, not unwillingness to serve in a strange country, but his sense of patriotism, his love of Israel: if Nineveh were destroyed, and her power broken, then Israel would be safe from the marauder from the north. And he was afraid lest, knowing God's merciful heart, he might spare Nineveh, and so open up once again the possibility that Israel might yet be devastated by invasion and conquest.

We need, however, to see Jonah's motivation in its full light and implications. What it means is that Jonah was really trying to 'twist God's arm', and manipulate him and his purposes so as to save Israel from Nineveh's might. It was his failure to do this that put him so much out of countenance. This is what explains his extreme displeasure, revealed in chapter four. It is as if Jonah were saying, "O God, you have done the wrong thing, you have spoiled everything by showing mercy to Nineveh. You have put your own people in jeopardy of their lives."

Several observations may be made about this. For one thing, it seems that Jonah could not see any other way for this danger to Israel to be avoided. He could not see, blinded as he was by his own blinkered attitudes, that God could be trusted to care for his own, and look after their interests, even if Nineveh were spared. No one is ever the worse for God showing mercy to cruel tyrants. He could not see that God was big enough to deal with such a problem. One thinks of the words of the Scottish paraphrase,

> Art thou afraid his power shall fail
> When comes thy evil day?
> And can an all-creating arm
> Grow weary or decay?
> Supreme in wisdom as in power
> the Rock of Ages stands...

Can we really think that such a God is going to be hard-pressed to protect his own? Jonah needed, and we also need, to see the impropriety - and the hazard - of accusing God of making mistakes.

For another thing, by his action and attitudes Jonah was interfering with the Divine purposes in the world. And something of the enormity of this must surely have been stirring in Jonah's heart and conscience, contributing to his 'out-of-jointness' with God. It reminds one of the statement made, with some wit and with a great deal of perception and truth, that there are "people who want to serve God, but in an advisory capacity only." But God does not need our advice. He does not need us to tell him what to do or what not to do. He is God the Lord, and we had better remember it. We are but men.

Furthermore, we should consider well the prophet's attitude expressed in 4:2,3: "I knew that thou art a gracious God, and merciful, slow to anger, and of great kindness, and repentest thee of the evil. Therefore now, O Lord, take, I beseech thee, my life from me..." Well! And Jonah was sorry, and angry, that he was such a God. Is it surprising, with such a spirit within him, that he was so completely out of sorts, cast down and depressed? As we said at the beginning of this study, some people make things very difficult for themselves. It is little wonder that the Lord said to him, "Doest thou well to be angry?"

This is not to say, however, that Jonah was conscious of why he was angry, or that his anger was against God. We have all sorts of defensive mechanisms that we build around us, to keep the truth from ourselves; and it is salutary that this word is in the Scriptures and that God put his finger on the real issue. Of course we do not articulate our anger with God: it is usually other people who get the brunt of it. When we feel ill done by, or neglected, when we are so critical of others for what they are supposed to have done to us, it is really God we are angry with. Behind and beyond the circumstances that crowd in upon us to hurt and distress us there is a deep resentment against God for allowing them, but woe betide anyone who happens to be near at the time, for they get the full force of it.

One recalls the story of a lady who had stopped going to church, bitter against God at the loss of her son in the war. She spoke of how she had given her son, and how God had been cruel to her. How could God be a God of love to have done this to her? In discussion about this, her minister told me: "Given her son? If she had given her son, she would have been healed of her grief years ago." She lost her son, but she did not give him; not even when he was taken away did she give him. If only she had let go! But she had not let go, and because she had not done so, the thing had festered in her heart for years, and it had ruined her life. There are many thousands whose sons were taken from them. They have sorrow in their hearts, even to this day, but they do not have the bitterness, the resentment, the querulousness against God because they have accepted the situation, and come to terms with their grief.

It is possible to nurse a grief or other misfortune in such a way that it develops into a canker, and becomes a resentment against God that will colour all our outlook, and we will become unlovely, unpleasant, bitter people, and we will just want to die, like Jonah. Such an attitude will slowly destroy us, and destroy the hope of anything true and fine and worthwhile in our lives. We will be dying by degrees, without knowing it.

Now let us see how God dealt with him. The first thing to notice is the patient forbearance which he showed to the prophet. "Doest thou well," he said, "to be angry?" We could perhaps paraphrase this and say, "Is this really fair, Jonah? Come now, are you justified in being angry with me like this?" This is one of the extraordinary things about the book: its revelation of the living God and his unaccountable forbearance and patience towards this recalcitrant, obsessed prophet, who had so many blind spots and so many chips on his shoulder about life. What an unlovely character he was because of these things, and how patient God was with him!

Furthermore, there was the parable of the gourd. God prepared a gourd for him, that it might be a shadow over his head, to deliver him from his grief. What we need to see here is the sweet reasonableness of God's dealings with Jonah. Two things may be said about this, and the first is that this is what God is like. He is so sweetly reasonable with us in our difficulties, with all the chips we have on our shoulders, with our utter blindness.

The second is that he is also concerned to woo Jonah by sweet reasonableness to a position where he can see how unreasonable it is to bear this grudge about Nineveh and about God's dealings with it. This is really very daring of God. His answer to Jonah's obsessional attitude, his disorientation, his completely wrong attitude to life, was to reason him out of it. He provided the gourd, and he arranged circumstances in which he awakened a feeling of pity and sorrow in Jonah's heart about the gourd that had been unkindly eaten away by the caterpillars. Jonah was sorry, not only that he had lost his shade in the pitiless heat of the noonday sun, but also that this thing had happened to such a lovely plant. God saw the pity welling up in Jonah's heart and said, "Jonah, you are taking pity on this gourd, on which you expended no labour; how much more should I be allowed to show pity on this people whom I have created, who are made in my image. Do you not see how unreasonable you are being?"

The issue, then, in Jonah's case, in his dark and gloomy depression of spirit, was a spiritual one; and God dealt with him, ministering gently to him in sweet reasonableness till all the resentment and hatred and bigotry drained away, and he got himself sorted out, and his priorities re-ordered, and his emphasis put in the proper place.

But for so long Jonah refused to accept the situation! This is why there is always a need to come to terms with oneself as well as with one's situation because the corrosive and destroying power of resentment in the heart, for whatever cause, or however justified, is absolutely deadly. Not until there is an acceptance of the will of God can there be real deliverance. Not merely submission to his will, but acceptance of it - and a recognition that because this is how God has ordained it, it must be best; and faith rises to lay hold of this in a positive sense. Until then, we shall go about with a chip on our shoulder, which will affect everything in our lives and everything we do, and it will alienate us from people, because even if they do not know our circumstances they see the end-product, and it is a very ugly sight.

If, then, we are secretly disappointed with God, like Jonah, and angry with him that he will not dance to our tune; if we have, as it were, set the stage and the way we want things; and if we are so obsessed with the way we want things that we are not prepared to see what everyone else sees, we are going to be thoroughly out-of-sorts and out-of-joint and the outlook is likely to be very poor indeed. This is how it was with Jonah, and it is as well that we should see what a critical ground this is to take. "O God, I told you so. Was not this my saying when I was yet in my country? This is why I fled before you. I knew you were a gracious God, and I did not want you to be gracious to Nineveh, I wanted you to destroy it. I wanted you to do it my way." God help us if that is the attitude we sometimes adopt! With such a resentment corroding our spirits, how good and kind God can be in his dealings with us, how gentle and compassionate!

We could put it this way: Jonah was too valuable and precious to God for him to acquiesce in Jonah's attitude to himself. It was as if God were saying, "Come on now Jonah, you mean too much to me for me to allow you to continue in this disorientated state. Think with me, open your eyes, and see how wrong this attitude of yours is, and how much it is hurting you. Jonah, my will is bigger than your patriotism, my will is bigger than this thing which is inexpressibly dear to you, and you dare not let that inexpressibly dear thing come in conflict with it."

The book of Jonah ends without indicating whether the prophet's conflict and depression were finally resolved; but we dare to hope that the sweet reasonableness and gentleness of God prevailed over his resentment. If this be so, can we doubt that it will also avail for us?

8

THE WEEPING PROPHET

Jeremiah 8:22: "Is there no balm in Gilead; is there no physician there?"

We turn now to a consideration of a servant of God who felt, more than most of his generation, the vast sadness and sorrow that attend a contemplation of the tragedy and horror of war and violence. He gave voice to his distress in a remarkable and deeply moving series of utterances in the heart of his prophecy, in chapters 9-20.

Jeremiah has sometimes been called the weeping prophet - and with justification, for his writing is full of tears, as we shall see when we look at the remarkable series of soliloquies in these chapters.

First of all, however, a brief word about the background of his prophecy is necessary. Jeremiah prophesied, as the opening verses of his book tell us, in the reigns of Josiah, Jehoakim and Zedekiah. These were the twilight years of Judah, the southern kingdom, before Babylon took them all into captivity and razed Jerusalem to the ground. It was a time heavy with crisis and impending doom. The land had passed through very troublous times, with crisis after recurrent crisis, and always there was the threat of war, with growing violence and godlessness in society. One scarcely needs to make the point that our situation today, nationally and internationally, is very much like that confronted by Jeremiah. There is a word in Romans 10:21, quoted by Paul from Isaiah: "All day long I have stretched forth my hands unto a disobedient and gainsaying people."

If that was true in Isaiah's time, it was even more true in Jeremiah's. This 'all day long' is echoed eloquently and very movingly in Jeremiah 8:18 - 9:2, in words that reveal the heartbreak of the prophet, as he weeps over the sin and the shame of the people, "Oh that my head were waters, and mine eyes a fountain of tears, that I might weep day and night and day for the slain of the daughter of my people."

Now - and this is the history of the time - Josiah, in whose reign Jeremiah began to prophesy, was a good king, indeed one of the very best kings of Judah in the gathering darkness of the age, and he had initiated widespread movements of reform in the land. And to begin with, from what we can gather from the history of the time in 2 Kings, Jeremiah was welcoming of his reforms, and had high hopes of them. The book of the law was recovered in the Temple, and this led to widespread spiritual awakening and renewal. But as time went on, it seems to have become clear to the prophet that the work of reformation was not deep enough - it was too little, too late - and it was this that brought so much desolation to his spirit.

King Josiah was killed, while still quite young, at the battle of Megiddo in 608 B.C. - it has been called the Flodden Field of Judah - and this was the beginning of the end for the nation; the downward path from that time onwards became increasingly evident. This is demonstrated in a graphic and indeed dramatic way in the later chapters of Jeremiah's prophecy. In 36:1ff., a passage which belongs to the early years of the reign of Jehoiakim, Josiah's son, we read of a significant and fateful encounter with that ill-starred monarch. Jeremiah was commanded by the Lord to write in book form all the words that he had spoken to the nation, from the days of Josiah until that time, and summoned his servant Baruch to read them in the Temple on the fast day. This made a deep impression on many of the nobles, who forthwith took the book for the king to read. Jehoiakim, however, treated it with contempt, mutilated it with a penknife and cast it in the fire.

The significance of this incident is underlined by the fact that it took place 'in the fifth year of Jehoiakim' (36:9), in 603 B.C.. This was the year in which another great and decisive battle took place, at Carchemish, in which Nebuchadnezzar of Babylon destroyed the might of Egypt, to become the supreme world power, making his eventual attack on Judah simply a matter of time. It was in this context, and in the face of the now ominous threat from Babylon, that the hapless Jehoiakim refused so contemptuously the word of the Lord. The comment in Jeremiah 36:24, "Yet they were not afraid, nor rent their garments, neither the king, nor any of his servants that heard all these words," underlines the fateful sense of nemesis overhanging the nation at that time. Where God's holy Word is held at a discount, despised, rejected and derided, things inevitably begin to happen in the national and international sphere. Such is the scenario of Jeremiah's prophecy, and the background against which we can best appreciate the mood expressed in the great soliloquies it contains. Consider the following:

"The Lord made it known to me and I knew; then thou didst show me their evil deeds. But I was like a gentle lamb led to the slaughter. I did not know it was against me they devised schemes, saying, 'Let us destroy the tree with its fruit, let us cut him off from the land of the living, that his name be remembered no more." (Jer. 11:18,19, RSV)

"Righteous art thou, O Lord, when I complain to thee; yet I would plead my case before thee. Why does the way of the wicked prosper? Why do all who are treacherous thrive? Thou plantest them, and they take root; they grow and bring forth fruit; thou art near in their mouth and far from their heart.' " (Jer. 12:1,2, RSV)

"O thou hope of Israel, its saviour in time of trouble, why shouldst thou be like a stranger in the land, like a wayfarer who turns aside to tarry for a night? Why shouldst thou be like a man confused, like a mighty man who cannot save? Yet thou, O Lord, art in the midst of us, and we are called by thy name; leave us not." (Jer. 14:8,9,RSV)

"Woe is me, my mother, that you bore me, a man of strife and contention to the whole land! I have not lent, nor have I borrowed, yet all of them curse me. So let it be, O Lord, if I have not entreated thee for their good, if I have not pleaded with thee on behalf of the enemy in the time of trouble and in the time of distress!" (Jer. 15:10,11, RSV)

"O Lord, thou knowest; remember me and visit me, and take vengeance for me on my persecutors. In thy

forbearance take me not away; know that for thy sake
I bear reproach... Why is my pain unceasing, my
wound incurable, refusing to be healed? Wilt thou be
to me like a deceitful brook, like waters that fail?"
(Jer. 15:15,18, RSV)

"Heal me, O Lord, and I shall be healed; save me,
and I shall be saved; for thou art my praise. Behold,
they say to me, 'Where is the word of the Lord? Let
it come!' I have not pressed thee to send evil, nor
have I desired the day of disaster, thou knowest; that
which came out of my lips was before thy face. Be
not a terror to me; thou art my refuge in the day of
evil." (Jer. 17:14-17, RSV)

"Then they said, 'Come, let us make plots against
Jeremiah, for the law shall not perish from the priest,
nor counsel from the wise, nor the word from the
prophet. Come, let us smite him with the tongue, and
let us not heed any of his words.' Give heed to me,
O Lord, and hearken to my plea. Is evil a recompense
for good? Yet they have dug a pit for my life." (Jer.
18:18-20, RSV)

"O Lord, thou hast deceived me, and I was
deceived; thou art stronger than I, and thou hast
prevailed. I have become a laughing-stock all the
day; everyone mocks me. For whenever I speak, I
cry out, I shout, 'Violence and destruction!' For the
word of the Lord has become for me a reproach and
derision all day long. If I say, 'I will not mention him,
or speak any more in his name,' there is in my heart
as it were a burning fire shut up in my bones, and I
am weary with holding it in, and I cannot. For I hear
many whispering. Terror is on every side! 'Denounce
him! Let us denounce him!' say all my familiar

friends, watching for my fall. 'Perhaps he will be deceived, then we can overcome him, and take our revenge on him.' " (Jer. 20:7-10, RSV)

"Cursed be the day on which I was born! The day when my mother bore me, let it not be blessed! Cursed be the man who brought the news to my father, 'A son is born to you,' making him very glad. Let that man be like the cities which the Lord overthrew without pity; let him hear a cry in the morning and an alarm at noon, because he did not kill me in the womb; so my mother would have been my grave, and her womb for ever great. Why did I come forth from the womb to see toil and sorrow, and spend my days in shame?" (Jer. 20:14-18, RSV)

It would be difficult to find a more deeply moving description of the inner anguish and agony suffered by a sensitive heart and spirit, as he passed through the dark valley of perplexity, isolation and despair, worn out and exhausted by the continued strain and pressure of a crisis that seemed to have no resolution or ending. Not many of us may be called to pass through such circumstances as he did, but our own dark experiences may well produce in us the anguish and distress that he suffered, and we can surely empathise with his deepest feelings as expressed in such outbursts of distress.

For one thing, we may think of the deep sense of distress that many - and perhaps especially older people - experience at the thought of the evil and the violence of our world, and the pain and anguish that this brings to their minds and hearts, and the tears they often shed at the mystery of things - the dark depression that comes upon them and the sense, almost, of outrage that fills them as they listen to the news and read the newspapers about the terrible things that happen day by day.

This reflects the insecurity and uncertainty of our society today. It is certainly not by accident that elderly people will not open the doors of their homes in the darkness of the evening hours, because they are afraid. They look back over the years and realise that the world of their earlier days was a much safer and much less threatening place than it is today. We should not underestimate the effect that this can have, and the contribution it makes to the incidence of anxiety and depression in the older generation.

Furthermore, there is the added and desolating sense of things not getting any better, but rather worse. This must surely have been part of Jeremiah's distress, with the additional burden of continued inability and failure to do anything to remedy the situation. This must sometimes have been almost more than he could bear, bringing dark and obstinate questionings that seemed likely to undermine his faith. "Why is God as a stranger in the land? Why is my pain perpetual, and my wound incurable?" his heart was crying in anguish. This was the Slough of Despond indeed!

The first sense of oppression was compounded by two further considerations. On the one hand, Jeremiah was deeply conscious of the terrible perversity of sin. In an impressive passage (Jer. 17:1-9) the prophet sets out in stark contrast the only two alternatives open to his people: either trust in the Lord or trust in the arm of the flesh. In the last analysis, the Scriptures do not allow of a middle position, a kind of innocuous and harmless 'half-way house'. The man who trusts in man is not merely mistaken in his confidence, he is cursed, because that trust in man represents a revolt against the true and living God. The dilemma that faced Jeremiah was this: if the way of life, trusting in the Lord, is so blessed and fruitful, and the way of cursing is so dire and terrible, why does man choose the latter rather than the former? The answer can lie only in the sheer perversity of the human heart, which is 'deceitful above all things, and desperately wicked.'

That his people, who had lived through such days of opportunity in the time of Josiah's reformation, and had had the good word of the Lord proclaimed to them, should have in such perversity of heart chosen the dark and the evil, left him a heartbroken man.

On the other hand, his soul was deeply exercised and vexed by the mystery of a providence that, against all the assurances in Scripture to the contrary, seemed to favour evil men, or at least be unmindful of their evil, for they continued to walk smoothly and at ease (Jer. 12:1ff). Jeremiah knew that the Divine Law taught that obedience to it brings blessing whereas disobedience brings cursing and judgment, but his experience was so different; he was suffering, not prospering, for his faithfulness to God.

Jeremiah was too deep and serious a man to doubt the validity of the Law, and doubtless he recognised, as Job did before him, that life cannot always be neatly tied up and pigeon-holed. He knew that there are many times when the stock answer (such as those given by Job's comforters) are the right ones but that there are some occasions when these do not fit, and are not appropriate. When this happens, we must be prepared, in recognising that a deeper dimension is at work, to remain in darkness and not know the answer to the 'Why's' of life.

The answer God gave to Jeremiah in his anguish and distress was a twofold one, involving both a shorter term, interim prescription, and also a longer term assurance. These, though widely different in emphasis, may be seen to be integrally connected to one another.

The more immediate answer to the prophet's questionings is given in the well known words,

If thou hast run with the footmen, and they have wearied thee, then how canst thou contend with horses? And if in the land of peace, wherein thou trustedst, they wearied thee, then how wilt thou do in the swelling of Jordan? (Jer. 12:5)

The words have been rendered variously in modern translations, but their general sense is clear. It was a striking answer given to his wistful and perplexed questionings about the Lord's dealings with men. It was not comfort, not assurance, but - in the words of one commentator - 'a stern summons to a more heroic and strenuous conflict with the forces arrayed against the truth'. It is as if God were saying to him, "There is worse to come yet, Jeremiah. Do not ask for an easier time; pray to be made strong enough to face all that will yet befall you." A stark, blunt, almost harsh word - yet we cannot doubt but that it was a word full of grace for him, and, doubtless one that would spur him to the kind of heroism that God was requiring of him. God knows what we are capable of, far better than we ourselves know, and we need not suppose otherwise than that Jeremiah rose to the challenge magnificently.

The longer term answer given to the prophet - and this must surely be set over against his sense of the failure and rejection of his prophetic message, and the absence of any response from those who heard it - was that after all his agonised and anguished outpourings and indeed in the midst of them, the word of the Lord began to come through to him with assurance. It was as if God said to him, "Yes, Jeremiah, these are indeed dark days, but I am still God. I have not abandoned my people, but I will punish them; yet I will not make a full end, I will bless them through the judgment that I bring upon them." This was the gleam of light that saved Jeremiah from utter despair. And as the message of the prophecy unfolds, a new note begins to be struck, and he actually comes to the point where he speaks of a new covenant that God would make with his people. Speaking of the slow and imperceptible change of emphasis in the prophecy, one commentator writes,

The tone of the prophecy gradually begins to change. Hope enters. There is the promise of the provision of faithful pastors, of a return from exile, of restoration after judgment, and of the coming of the Messiah himself. The preservation of the remnant is assured. The judgment of the oppressor, God's instrument of chastisement, is also sure. The note of hope becomes dominant. God's purpose will be accomplished, and will culminate in the making of a new covenant. His people will be inwardly changed and live out the will of God.

With such a bedrock promise and assurance, Jeremiah was enabled to hold on, and to hold out, to the end. To be sure, many dark days were yet to come, in which he saw his grim prophecies fulfilled to the letter as his people continued in their wilful and stubborn refusal of his message, and in which he himself underwent unspeakable persecution and torture. Yet it is impressive that, in the gathering darkness of that doom-laden time, prior to the final onslaught upon Jerusalem by Nebuchadnezzar of Babylon, Zedekiah the king sent to the prophet whom men had despised, rejected and held in contempt for so long, to ask for counsel of him: "Is there any word from the Lord?" This was surely a recognition on the king's part, in spite of himself, of where the truth really lay, and of who could really speak for God. It was a vindication of Jeremiah's whole ministry, and of the stand he had taken for God.

Here, then, is a man deeply sensitive in spirit, who went through agony, anguish and doubt about the mysteries and tragedies of life questioning God, rueing the day he was born, and bearing his burden in an isolation and loneliness that was almost more than he could bear. Yet, in the darkness and desolation of his spirit he was made conscious by the word of the Lord that sin and evil do not have the last word in human experience, and made receptive to the message that, in spite of everything, God would fulfil his purpose in his people.

Jeremiah's experience in his visit to the potter's house (Jer. 18:1ff) assured him that the sovereignty of God was the one overwhelming reality, eclipsing all other, and that it was a sovereignty of grace, and that it was possible, even out of the disastrous marring of the vessel in the potter's hands, which the prophet could see all around him in the nation of his day, for God to make another vessel for his glory.

From the long term point of view, this in fact was done; from beyond the tragedy and fiery furnace of the Captivity, God took up his people again, and in spite of all their intractible perversity fulfilled his purposes in them, and in the fulness of the time brought forth from them his Redeemer. This was what comforted the prophet and assuaged the anguish and distress of his heart. The vision, so far as he was concerned was 'Yet for an appointed time;' but he had seen it and it led him into peace, and fortified him against all that he was yet to bear before he reached the end of his pilgrimage.

Faith, as the apostle puts it, is the substance of things hoped for, the evidence of things not seen, and it must have gladdened the heart of God to see his servant so trusting in his Word even in his anguish and heartbreak. What a challenge this is to us also, 'in the maddening maze of things, when tossed by storm and flood,' to cling to the fixed ground of the promises of God, and to lay hold of what is pledged and promised to us in his faithful Word.

9

DISCOURAGEMENT IN THE WORK

Ezra 4:4: "The people of the land weakened the hands of the people of Judah, and troubled them in building."

We turn now to the post-exilic period of Old Testament history, and to the story of the fortunes of God's people after their return from exile in Babylon, when they began to rebuild the devastated temple in Jerusalem.

The Book of Ezra, which recounts this story, describes in its first six chapters the return of the exiles in the reign of Cyrus, in 538 B.C., under Sheshbazzar, Zerubbabel and Joshua the High Priest. It is only in the second part of the book, chapters 7-12, that Ezra himself comes on the scene, in 458 B.C., some 80 years later than the events recorded in the first part of the book.

On their return to Jerusalem (3:1-7), the altar of burnt offering was erected, offerings were made, the Feast of Tabernacles was celebrated, and in the second month of the second year, work began on the Temple itself (3:8-13). As soon as work began on the Temple, adversaries began to interfere (4:1-5), and to frustrate the work of building. The opposition continued in such a way that the work was consistently and persistently hindered and finally stopped. This state of affairs continued until the reign of King Darius.

The enemies of the Jews had their own reasons for opposing their return to Palestine (one can think of the same kind of problems in Palestine in our own time) and by bringing an evil report concerning them to the emperor, succeeded in having the work of rebuilding stopped. The people, it appears, lost heart, but Haggai and Zechariah stirred them up to resume the work on the Temple. Opposition again appeared, and the matter was referred to Darius (5:1-17) who searched for Cyrus' decree, examined it, and then decreed that the work could proceed. This was decisive and in 516-515 B.C. the Temple was completed and dedicated, and the Passover and Feast of Unleavened Bread celebrated (6:1-22).

It will help us in our study if we look at something of the background to these first years after the return from the Exile. In chapter 3 we read of the establishment of the altar of God, the celebration of the Feast of Tabernacles, and the laying of the foundation of the Temple. This order was in itself significant from a symbolic point of view: before the laying of the Temple foundations there had to be the establishing of the altar, reminding us that before there can be any rebuilding of waste places, men must first of all themselves get right with God.

The returned exiles began well and properly, then; and the literal return from Babylon to Jerusalem was matched by a spirit of return from backsliding to God. It was in this spirit that they set about the work of rebuilding.

It does not need much imagination to realise what

a tremendous enthusiasm must have gripped these men, as they started to rebuild, and what a moving experience it must have been for them, especially for those among them who were older, who had seen the first Temple and known its glory (cf 3:12,13).

Scarcely had the work begun, however, when trouble came. The adversaries of Judah and Benjamin, on hearing about the rebuilding, came with offers of help in the work. But Zerubbabel, mindful of the problems that had arisen in pre-exilic days through association with those who were not God's people, refused their help in no uncertain manner. This led to a concerted campaign of harassment designed to frustrate and prevent the work of rehabilitation to which the exiles had committed themselves. This is the message of the 4th chapter of the book of Ezra.

There are two things to note here. The first is that in any work of God opposition is inevitable. It is something we all have to come to terms with, in the very fact that we are Christians at all. The second thing is that such opposition can, and does, go on and on, and it is very easy eventually to be worn down by it.

Ezra appears to sum up in this chapter all the opposition that the people of God experienced throughout the whole work of reconstruction, first with the Temple, and then with the building of the walls of Jerusalem in Nehemiah's time. This is the best way to understand what otherwise might seem to be a confused and confusing record. The simplest solution is to realise that Ezra is collating all the evidence of opposition and hindrance throughout the whole history of the returned exiles, in all four reigns, through a period of seventy years or more. It is as if he were pointing out that this kind of opposition was not an isolated phenomenon, but went on all the time the children of Israel were occupied in building. This explains why in verses 1-5 the opposition is to the building of the Temple, whereas in verses 6-23 the opposition is to the building of the walls of the city, which took place at a later stage.

What we are meant to understand is that letters of complaint were constantly being sent to the court of these various kings against the Jews, but in fact only one of these letters is recorded for us, that to Artaxerxes, much later than Zerubbabel's time. All along, and again and again, this opposition continued. At times it stopped the work altogether. From the historical point of view, then, verses 1-5 and 24 belong together, and verses 6-23 constitute a parenthesis, so to speak, which illustrates, from Ezra's point of view, that this work of hindrance and opposition continued throughout the long period in which the work of reconstruction was being carried forward, first with the Temple, then later, under Nehemiah, with the building of the walls of Jerusalem.

Such, then, is the scenario for our study: the pressures of opposition that came upon the people of God which, as they continued, brought about a cessation of the work of rebuilding for a period of some 16 years, from the time of the Return in 538 B.C. to the second year of Darius I in 522 B.C..

This is something that is surely relevant in all sorts of ways in the Christian life and in Christian work. In so many different ways we can experience the frustrations, and hindrances, and oppositions of the enemy. We never seem to get out of the bit, and often advance seems to be completely halted, and out of the question altogether.

Perhaps in our experience the opposition has come at the stage of the rebuilding of the broken altar of God. We have wanted to rebuild, and the enemy has been relentless in hindering us, and it is here that the discouragement has come. We have tried honestly and sincerely but the pressures have been so great, and the adversary has seemed to put paid to our efforts. Or, perhaps, it is further on, in the laying of the foundations - in the teaching of a Sunday School class, or Bible Class, for example, working with young people - that we seem to be making no impression, and no advance seems possible. Or, perhaps, it is some inward battle that we are fighting, which we recognise as all-important for all that we are engaged in, and we are not making any headway, but even losing ground. What do we do in such circumstances? Give up in discouragement and despair, admit defeat? Or fight on, gritting our teeth, and getting down to work, in the consciousness that a great and effectual door stands open for us, as it did for the Jews?

Here, then, was a situation of dark discouragement and low-spiritedness for the people of God, the desolate feeling of wanting to 'give up'. It was all so different from the first enthusiasms of earlier days. One wonders whether this is one of the things the prophet Habbakuk had in mind when he prayed, "O Lord, revive thy work in the midst of the years" - the middle years when the first flush of enthusiasm has given way to the steady plodding of later years. How easy to become discouraged then!

This is how it was with the returned exiles: things had turned out so very differently from what they had anticipated, the early glow had faded, they had lost heart, and dark discouragement had laid hold upon them.

But one of the problems and dangers about becoming discouraged and losing heart is that you lose something else also: you lose your testimony. This is precisely what happened with these returned exiles. It is not in fact stated in so many words in Ezra 4-5, although perhaps implied, but it is very clearly indicated in the writings of the prophets Haggai and Zechariah, especially the former, whom God raised up to help them back to a better and more positive spirit. One has only to read Haggai 1:1 ff. to see this. It is clear that complacency and apathy developed from the discouragement and low-spiritedness into which the exiles had fallen. We may notice in passing that low-spiritedness does provide a fertile ground for the seeds of spiritual apathy and complacency to grow, take root and flourish. Sometimes, too, when the low-spiritedness abates, the apathy and the complacency remain.

Perhaps they were easily discouraged, and had a low threshold, so far as fighting spirit was concerned? One can understand this too: a people who have been in captivity for generations do not have much heart in them. And when things began to go wrong for them - poor harvests, economic stringency, and pressure - they crumpled, and fell into the doldrums spiritually.

We look, then, at Haggai's prophecy. The final verse of Ezra 4 says, "They ceased the work of the house of God which is in Jerusalem. So it ceased unto the second year of the reign of Darius king of Persia." The opening words of Haggai's prophecy are, "In the second year of Darius the king, in the sixth month, in the first day of the month, came the word of the Lord by Haggai the prophet unto Zerubbabel, the son of Shealtiel, governor of Judah, and to Joshua the son of Josedech, the high priest." This identifies the situation in which Haggai exercised his ministry: sixteen years after the standstill of the work, when the first adversaries persuaded the king of Persia to halt the whole proceedings.

The extent to which discouragement and its resultant apathy had affected the people is clearly underlined in Haggai's forthright challenge, as he exposed to the people the real nature of their problem. The mandate they had been given by Cyrus of Persia when he released them from their captivity was to go back and build their Temple and their city, but now, sixteen years on, they were saying, "The time is not come that the Lord's house should be built." What price now the enthusiasm of the earlier years? These were the people who had celebrated the Feast of Tabernacles with such joy, dedication and expectation, and now they were sunk in apathy. This was what discouragement had done to them. And the prophet summoned them to consider their ways, as we indeed must try to do in the light of what is said by the prophet.

Was there some kind of misunderstanding of the ways of God in them that they became so discouraged by opposition? Did they really expect everything to be 'plain sailing'? Is it realistic to expect this in the work of God? And were they not perhaps thinking romantically of the past? It is possible to have romantic notions of the way God works, and romantic expectations of how he should work today. We sometimes sing F.W. Faber's words:

101

Workman of God! O lose not heart,
But learn what God is like, ...

But do we know what he is like, and how he works?

An illustration may help here: one thinks of the post-war years, 1945-50, and the expectation of revival and national renewal in the hearts of many of God's people at that time. How many prayed and cried to God and expected him, after the horrors and upheaval of six years of war, to visit his people in awakening! But revival did not come. Was there not discouragement and disheartening, as the years passed and we did not see our heart's desire? Ah, God is other than we think, as the hymn says.

One recalls the graphic story in the book of Exodus, when the people of God were in captivity in Egypt, and their prayers and cries seemed to go unheard for so long. The heavens seemed as brass, and they must have thought that God had forgotten to be gracious. But even as they thus languished in discouragement and despair, prayer had already been answered, for a baby had been born into a Levite home, and miraculously preserved and nurtured, and prepared for God's service as the deliverer of his people. Moses was born, but it was forty years before they realised that God had answered their prayers. Yet he was God's answer to the need of the time.

May this not have something to say to us in our situation of need in the land today? For what has been happening in these last forty years is that babies have been born, and young men have grown up, and the hand of God has come upon them, and there is a consciousness in their hearts that they have been born in answer to the prayers of these earlier days. Lives have been changed and transformed and a band of men - and thank God, they are a growing number! - whose hearts God has touched, have gone out, and will yet go out, into the work of God for the rebuilding of the waste places of our land. And what of the children and young people now in our care and under our nurture? May the Lord not have purposes for their lives also in his service, at home and abroad?

What if this is the way God has chosen to work in our time? Should we be insensitive to it? We should never be discouraged - that is the message that comes through to us in these days, and it is reinforced when we consider how it was in Ezra's time. First of all, there was the inexorable challenge from the prophet Haggai (1:7-11), which jolted them out of their complacency and apathy; this was followed by the immediate response of Zerubbabel and Joshua, who led the people into a new dedication in a re-commencement of the building work, with new hope and renewed vision stimulated by the Word of God (Haggai 1:12- 15).

If we look at the dating given in Haggai 1:1 and 15 it will be seen that in a matter of little more than three weeks the situation was entirely transformed. The reaction and response to Haggai's speaking forth of the Word of God was practically immediate. What follows in the second chapter of the prophecy indicates that, once the people got going, words of encouragement were given them to keep them going. Such is the pattern. God is not always hammering at men; when we obey him he encourages us, with the words, "Behold I am with you; fear ye not."

The subsequent history of this time serves to give

substance to this Divine exhortation. It is true that the opposition of the enemies of God's people was renewed against them; but there was a difference this time, as we see from a comparison of Haggai's prophecy with the opening chapters of Zechariah. For Zechariah brought "good words and comfortable words" (1:13) to the people, proclaiming the Divine purposes of grace and mercy for Jerusalem (1:16). This is underlined even more graphically in one of his later prophecies (4:2 ff.), in which the vision of the golden candlestick is interpreted to Zechariah as representing the power of the Spirit of God at work on behalf of his people. The prophecy continues (4:7): "Who art thou, O great mountain? before Zerubbabel thou shalt become a plain." What is the mountain referred to? It is the mountain of opposition before which the returned exiles were trembling and quailing, in their fear that the building of the Temple was going to be stopped a second time. "Not so," says God. He is the God who sweeps mountains out of the way of his people, when his purposes are being fulfilled. "The hands of Zerubbabel have laid the foundation of this house; his hands shall also finish it" (4.9).

Such is the pattern when men become responsive and obedient to the Word of God. The coming of the Word of God into situations of discouragement and apathy is always fraught with incalculable consequences for good. It is the Divine Word alone that can give the inspiration needed for a forward movement. Given that, work will be done and walls will be rebuilt.

This is why, in the Christian life, it is so essential to cleave to the Divine Word, holding on to it, if need be in grim desperation even when - and especially when -

all around us seems to be giving way and there is little semblance of reality in our spiritual experience, when reading the Scriptures and trying to pray alike seem empty and futile. That is the danger point, the point at which black discouragement can turn to apathy. The words of Toplady's hymn have been a means of grace to many in such an experience:

When we in darkness walk,
Nor feel the heavenly flame,
Then is the time to trust our God,
And rest upon his Name.

Wait till the shadows flee;
Wait thy appointed hour;
Wait till the Bridegroom of thy soul
Reveals his love with power.

That is how it was in the post-exilic situation: in the glad providence of God two men were raised up to proclaim the Word of God to the people, and everything was changed. Let us likewise wait upon that Divine Word until God gives the times of refreshing that our generation so desperately needs.

Workman of God! O lose not heart!

10

THE DARK NIGHT OF THE SOUL

Matthew 11:3: "Art thou he that should come, or do we look for another?"

The New Testament Scriptures contain quite as many insights into the subject of Spiritual Depression as the Old, and we turn in this chapter to the experience of John the Baptist as recorded in Matthew 11:1 ff. and Luke 7:19 ff.. This is the record of a highly significant incident which affords a very important insight in to the general problem, for John the Baptist is seen in these passages in a dark mood of doubt and despondency, in the prison to which King Herod had committed him at the time our Lord's own public ministry began.

We look first of all at the context of the incident. It is fair to say at the outset that there have been different interpretations placed upon it. The first of these - and the one we are to follow in this study - is that John, who had been in prison for some time, had succumbed to a dark prison mood, in which serious doubts were assailing him about Jesus, perhaps accompanied by a

106

feeling that he had turned out a different Messiah from what he had expected.

Another interpretation is that John was himself quite sure of Jesus and his Messiahship, but that he wanted to convince his disciples that he was the Messiah, and that it was for this reason that he sent the disciples to Jesus with the question, "Art thou he that should come....? This is a view that was held by numbers of the early Church Fathers, but it seems to be decisively negatived by the fact that Jesus sent these disciples back with the message, "Go and tell John...." This seems to indicate that it was John, rather than his disciples, who needed the reassurance.

Yet another interpretations is that John was only now coming to faith in Jesus as the Messiah, and that what we have here is the dawning of faith in his soul. But this raises other problems, particularly in relation to the marvellous statement in John 1:29 where John gave the wonderful testimony to Jesus, "Behold. the Lamb of God, which taketh away the sin of the world." Clearly, John was sure of Jesus then, before ever he was cast into prison, and in the light of this it is scarcely feasible to speak of the dawning of his faith in this later situation.

Whatever construction is placed on the incident, however, it certainly represents an attitude of doubt and uncertainty, and this is its significance in relation to what Jesus says in answer to it. Let us look, then, at John, in the strange doubts and perplexities that were besetting him.

There are a number of reasons why he was in this state. For one thing, his ministry had lasted only a few months at the most. He had burst upon the land of

Israel like a meteor, and his preaching had scorched the conscience of the nation. On any estimate it was a tremendous ministry, making a telling impact at national level. He was an instrument in the hand of God for national awakening. Yet after a few short months he had been cast into prison and that ministry had been suddenly and, as it happened, finally cut short and brought to an end. The voice crying in the wilderness had been silenced, and God had allowed it. Was not this very mysterious, and would it not present a dark enigma to John? One has only to try to put oneself into John's position to realise the huge question mark that must have arisen in his mind. He was a man who from birth was filled with the Holy Ghost, for a work of God. He knew he was destined for such a work, and with what high hopes he must have brooded upon it in the wilderness until the day of his appearing to Israel. The initial impact of his ministry must surely have confirmed all these hopes - and now, after a matter of months, it was cut off.

His perplexity must have been further accentuated by the fact that Jesus himself seems to have done nothing about John's imprisonment. John had heard of the mighty works that Jesus had done, healing the sick, cleansing the leper, raising the dead. Was it beyond his power to set the prisoner free, especially such a prisoner? John must have known the Messianic prophecies of the Old Testament, not least Isaiah 61:1 about proclaiming "liberty to the captives, and the opening of the prison to them that are bound," and he seems to have been unable to square this in his thinking with his present continuing imprisonment.

Furthermore, Jesus was not, to his mind, fulfilling his

own prediction of Jesus as a coming Judge, with fan in his hand, and axe laid to the roots of the trees (Matt. 3:10 ff.). And where was the baptism of fire? This Messiah did not seem to fit what John had preached and prophesied concerning him.

All these things were causing John to question in his heart. There was so much he could not understand. And he sent his disciples to Jesus with the question, "Art thou he that should come? Have I been mistaken in what I have preached about you?" It may be that one would need to be a preacher fully to understand the tremendous pressure that this would put upon a man like John the Baptist. For a man to have a burning conviction in his heart about God and the things that God was going to do, and then for the whole situation to turn out very differently, is a terrible experience. That is why John the Baptist was passing through such a dark night of the soul. Here is a man questioning everything, his faith is under fire, and he does not know what to think.

This is an experience that can come to anyone, even when their problems are not John the Baptist's problems: circumstances have hedged them in, and so made impact upon their whole spiritual life that they are questioning and doubting, and in their questioning and doubting their hearts have entered into a bleakness and a darkness which is very frightening indeed. This is the point at which John the Baptist's experience, and our Lord's way of dealing with it, become relevant for us.

Our Lord's answer to John's disciples was this: "Go and show John again those things which ye do hear and see: the blind receive their sight, and the lame walk, the lepers are cleansed, and the deaf hear, the dead are raised up, and the poor have the gospel preached to them. And blessed is he, whosoever shall not be offended in me." It is important for us to try to assess the significance of these words: they have a great deal to teach us.

First of all, Jesus directed John's attention to his words and his works. What we may learn from this is that the way to come to faith, and the way for faith to be made strong, is to consider the deeds and words of Jesus. This is the biblical prescription, and it is echoed again and again in Scripture - to keep on considering them until their meaning and their majesty grip and master us, and master our doubts too, and bring us to a full conviction about him. Faith comes by hearing, as Paul says (Rom. 10:17), and hearing by the Word of God; and John says in his Gospel, "These are written (the deeds and words of Jesus) that ye may believe that Jesus is the Christ, and that believing ye might have life through his Name" (John 20:31).

The principle is echoed in some of our great hymns:

Send them thy mighty word to speak
Till faith shall dawn and doubt depart.

and

They preach his birth, his life, his Cross,
The love of his atonement.

When faith burns low, and minds are doubting and confused, here is the answer. Show men Christ's deeds and words, proclaim the Saviour. It is certainly not by accident that the Church's faith has dimmed and faltered as preaching Christ has been steadily displaced in our time. What need there is for a recovery of biblical preaching!

Furthermore, we should notice particularly in this situation when John's faith seemed to be clouded, Jesus said (following Matthew's account), "Show John again." We must not miss the significance of that word 'again'. There was no new prescription, when hearing did not seem to have worked at first, but a repetition of what he had already heard. It is hardly possible to over-emphasise the importance and significance of this. The Divine prescription for doubt and gloom is: the same message as before - nothing new!

In such a situation, of course, the temptation to seek something new is very real, and very natural, but it needs to be resisted. This is something that is very relevant for us today, when we are being plagued in the Church by people trying new things. They look at the Church's life, and in a snap judgment they say, "Such-and-such is not working, we must try something new." Anything new becomes the 'in' thing, which is tried, and for a time may create excitement and enthusiasm. And they think they have found the answer. But after a while it fades, and some other new thing has to be tried, then something else, and so on. So the Church staggers and reels under the impact of one new thing after another, endlessly trying to bolster its faith and revive its life. But this is not the prescription that the Bible gives, and it is not how Jesus dealt with John either. Rather, it was to be a reiteration and underlining of what he already knew, in the confidence and expectation that this would solve his problem.

There is an important principle enshrined in this: it is that of confidence and trust in the power of the Divine Word to do its gracious work in men's hearts. This is well illustrated in the record of Paul's missionary experience in the Acts of the Apostles, where it is said (14:3) that the Apostle, on encountering opposition against his preaching, did not change his approach, but continued with both message and method as before: "Long time therefore abode they speaking boldly in the Lord, which gave testimony unto the word of his grace, and granted signs and wonders to be done by their hands."

An illustration may serve to underline this further. A servant of God, greatly used during the last war among servicemen, recounts his experience with one young man whom he sought to lead to Christ. He spent a whole evening with him unfolding, as clearly and as simply as he knew how, the way of salvation in Christ. After two hours the young man shook his head and said, "I cannot see it." The man of God was discouraged and tempted to give up. Then he thought: "God has promised to bless his Word, and I have no other means of helping this man than the Word itself." What he did, therefore, was to go over again all that he had said to him from beginning to end. And he said, "It was wonderful to see the light dawning in that young man's eyes as the Spirit of God enlightened his darkness and brought him joy and peace in believing in the Lord Jesus." "Show him again," said Jesus.

Either we believe in the power of the Word of God to do its own work, or we do not. If we do not, we will perforce have to try something new; but if we believe in the power of that Word, and that it is the weapon which is mighty through God to the pulling down of strongholds, we shall continue to hold it forth. It is to this that our Lord's words to John bear witness.

This is why it is so important, as has already been emphasized, for us to hold on, and maintain our ground, when we are passing through dark and difficult times, when we are tempted to stop praying and stop reading the Scriptures because we feel that such exercises no longer have any meaning. At all costs we must 'go through the motions', and keep at them until the darkness subsides.

We should notice also, in the next place, that it is an appeal to reason that Jesus makes to John. He says, in effect, to John, "Think, man. What is Messiah supposed to do? Is not this that I am doing the work of Messiah? Can you not put two and two together, and see that I am he?" In this connection we need to recognise that Jesus, in giving John answer, couches what he says in messianic terms. John, in asking "Art thou he that should come?" himself uses messianic categories, for "he that should come" was a well-known messianic phrase used to describe the One who would meet man's deepest need. In the same way, Jesus answers John in kind, for the words and phrases he uses are filled with messianic ideas (cf. Isaiah 29:18 ff.; 35:5 ff.; 61:1 ff.). It is as if he has said, "What kind of Messiah were you thinking about, John? Is not this his work that I am doing?" Significantly, our Lord is doing here exactly what the apostle Peter later did on the Day of Pentecost, when he said, "This (that you see today) is that (prophesied in the Old Testament)." It was a question of his hearers 'putting two and two together', as our Lord was inviting John, in effect, to do.

It is to be noted that Jesus did not answer the questionings in John's mind. There was no explanation of why he was left to languish in prison - although after his disciples had left Jesus said something that indicated that the imprisonment was perhaps integral to the Divine purposes, and was fruitful in the work of the kingdom. Earlier, John had said, "He must increase, I must decrease," and this was literally happening. His imprisonment was perhaps the seedbed on which the flowers of the gospel were to come in the future. And even when John was bewailing his uselessness and the failure of his ministry, Jesus was calling him the greatest of the prophets, and the forerunner of the gospel. His martyrdom, indeed, was a foreshadowing of that Death that was to bring life to the world.

But Jesus gave him no explanation of it then, and for this reason: there are some things that will necessarily remain in the dark, some questions that will never be answered, some perplexities that will never be made clear. But these are never real barriers to faith. There is always enough evidence for faith to dawn, and doubt depart, in the word that is preached. Jesus, in saying, "Blessed is he that shall not be offended in me," is in fact implying "even if there are things you cannot understand, John, trust me. There is ample evidence for you to do that."

It is not always easy, of course, particularly when we are passing through such a time of despondency, to remain clear-eyed enough to appreciate what our Lord said to John, and says to us. We are tempted so often to say, "Unless you explain these things to me I cannot believe." But the Lord is not prepared to give explanations in such a situation. He knows it is not necessary. It is beside the point to say, "If only John the Baptist had heard what Jesus said about him, after his disciples returned to him: 'Among them that are born of women there hath not risen a greater than John the Baptist,' surely that would have encouraged him? Surely it would have been better if Christ had exercised his sovereign power and miraculously delivered him from prison?"

The fact is, John did not hear these words; and Jesus did not miraculously deliver him. That was not necessarily the best way, and could not be, if the prison was in the Divine plan for John. One recalls the story in the Gospels of the miracle of the stilling of the storm on the Sea of Galilee, when the disciples wakened the slumbering Jesus with the cry, "Carest thou not that we perish?" The Lord stilled that storm, but he also said, "Oh ye of little faith, wherefore didst thou doubt?" What if the miracle was a concession to the weakness of their faith, as the text seems to imply? What if Jesus wanted to teach them that they were safe in the midst of the storm when he was there, and that he did not need to perform the miracle to assure them of this, any more than John the Baptist needed a miraculous deliverance from prison?

The final point in our study is this. John was not delivered from prison; but it was his disciples that our Lord told to go and minister to their master. John's imprisonment was, it seems, for something immeasurably important in the purpose of God, and it was given to these unknown, unnamed disciples to minister comfort and encouragement to him. This, indeed, is a stewardship committed to all who name Christ's Name and one that can be wonderfully fulfilled by ordinary folk when, in the compassion and love of the Saviour, and with his gentleness and grace, they seek to minister words of encouragement to servants of God who are under pressure of different kinds, and passing through the Slough of Despond. Such a ministry will bear a rich harvest in an uplifted soul and a renewed spirit. We must not fail in that stewardship.

11

WILLING BONDAGE

John 5:6: "Wilt thou be made whole?"

One of our hymns contains the words,

Great Pilot of my onward way,
Thou wilt not let me drift,

and this must surely be a great encouragement to embattled believers as they try to cope with the pressures that beset them. But it is possible for us to allow ourselves to drift, and there needs to be an effort of will on our part to get ourselves going. As the hymn continues,

I feel the winds of God today,
Today my sail I lift.

We are, therefore, going to look at the place and function of the will in times of depression. At the outset, it needs to be made clear what is meant, and what is not meant, by this. Sometimes good folk, when they encounter others who are suffering from depression, say,

"Come on now, pull yourself together." There are, however, many genuine medical conditions, often described as 'nerves', which are responsible for much ill health and give rise to much unhappiness and mental suffering, in which it is not possible for people to 'pull themselves together'. It is not that they will not do so; they cannot, and it simply adds to their distress and anguish to be subjected to this kind of well-meaning but misguided - and sometimes insensitive - counsel.

This prompts the very natural question: "If this is the case, if it is pointless to exhort such people to pull themselves together, then what are we to say about the place and function of the will in the matter of depression?" This is a valid point, and hardly to be disputed, but what we have said relates to clinical or medical depression more than to the kind of spiritual malaise that we have been studying. What we are thinking of, rather, is the use one makes of the will in the context of the trials and pressures that come upon us, in terms of coping with them. It is in this sense that we now consider our Lord's words to the man at the Pool of Bethesda who, it will be remembered, was paralysed, and had been so for thirty-eight years. Jesus said to him, "Wilt thou be made whole? Do you want to be made better?" There is a sense in which these words present a complete paradox: the whole point about the man's condition was that he could not help himself; and yet, Jesus made a round and unequivocal challenge to his will. We need to look at this first of all for a little time, before going any further.

What do we suppose was the point and the purpose of Jesus' question? Was it not asking the obvious, to ask if he wanted to be made whole? Not so; it was not asking the obvious, and that for at least two very good and compelling reasons. On the one hand, the question that Jesus asked the man indicates a situation which is true to human psychology. We must bear in mind that he had been ill for thirty-eight years, and all these years he had known only infirmity and incapacity. We learn later that his own sin was involved in this; and one can readily imagine certain kinds of sin that could have caused physical paralysis. Imagine too, what all these years of infirmity must have done to his mind. The long, dreary continuance of his condition, year after year, must surely have robbed him of any expectation of betterment or of cure; one can think of the listlessness and the apathy that must have fallen upon him, with a mind and a heart so utterly resigned to his condition, so acquiescing in the inevitable, that dullness and despair had come upon his spirit. Christ's question introduced to him a new possibility, which had long since left him: he was being recalled to hope once again.

This has something to say to us, because, of course, in times of depression, this is precisely how people begin to think. If it goes on for a long time, they feel that they are never going to get out of the bit; and at this point there is the danger of real despair and real hopelessness. What Jesus said to the impotent man is a word that we can take to ourselves as one that recalls us to hope, and presents to us, as to him, a new possibility.

In the second place, even in the context of his misery and hopelessness, this question, 'Wilt thou be made whole?' still needed to be asked, for it is possible to prefer to remain sick, conscious though we be of need, rather than to be made whole again. Some invalids do not really want to get better: illness is a necessity for them; they would not really be happy unless they were miserable. In the spiritual sense, this is doubly true, and one readily sees parallels in the spiritual life. One thinks, for example, of the unwillingness of Nicodemus, or the woman of Samaria, to see what Jesus was getting at when he spoke to them. One of the solemn realities in spiritual issues is the fact of willing blindness in those who do not see the truth of the gospel. A part of Nicodemus did not want to see what Jesus meant when he said, "Ye must be born again," because seeing what he meant would have involved him in too much challenge, a challenge that he was not prepared to face.

When we translate this into the physical, mental, and psychological realms, we must recognise that sometimes people do not want to get better; having something wrong with them is a necessity for them, they need having something wrong with them as a prop in life. This is why Jesus asked this man, "Wilt thou be made whole?" He meant, "Do you really want to be made better?"

There is a considerable challenge in this, as may be seen when we think of some possible circumstances in which this is the truth of the situation. To take one illustration: it is an impressive experience to read the biography of the late Lord Reith, the first Governor General of the B.B.C.. The son of a Presbyterian Manse in Scotland, he had a deeply religious upbringing. In his young manhood, and indeed through most of his life, he laboured and suffered under a kind of deep depression of spirit which took the form of a gloomy, almost pathological, sense of not being one of God's elect. He had the sense and conviction that, no matter what he did, he could never find salvation. This is simply a variation of the problem of the unpardonable sin, one of the most dark and distressing causes of spiritual depression. For a good part of his mortal life this giant of a man laboured under this gloomy and sometimes terrifying oppression of spirit, in which he was convinced that he was reprobate. But, and this is the significant point, he battled manfully - heroically, indeed - with that darkness, gritting his teeth as he grappled with it, refusing to allow the dark cloud upon his spirit to influence what he did - and how much he did in his life, and with his life! He refused to allow his disability to paralyse him, but in spite of it he battled through it to usefulness, and made a magnificent contribution to his day and generation.

Reith was a big man, of course, big physically and big in intellectual and moral stature; but what he did with his life illustrates what is meant by the use of the will, and its function, in the context of depression. He had a will to press on. And it is in this way that Christ challenges us, in the story of the man at the Pool of Bethesda, to let our minds operate. This is always a factor in the situation, a gritting of one's teeth, a rolling up of one's sleeves to do battle, a wrestling and grappling with one's distress, and a refusal to give in to it.

Another kind of problem lies in the difficulty, sometimes amounting to complete inability, that some people have in forgiving themselves for something that has happened in their lives. It is a common experience to find believers in a state of depression because of this. God has forgiven them, but they cannot forgive themselves, and every time they get down on their knees in prayer the problem rises up to overwhelm them. But this can develop into a luxury that we simply cannot afford in the spiritual life; and the battle then becomes 'will' and 'mind' versus 'feelings', and the luxury of misery.

In this context Christ's question "Wilt thou be made whole?" becomes very relevant. The deliverance is there for the taking, but so often we are simply not prepared to believe the love that God has for us; and as long as we refuse to forgive ourselves, our spiritual life is going to be paralysed. This becomes a real moral issue, and indeed a greater sin than the thing that we are grieving over. The truth of the matter is, it is very easy to become preoccupied with our sins and with the burden of the past. If God says, "Your sins and your iniquities will I remember no more," then we need not remember them any more. It is very impressive to see in the New Testament how little preoccupied with sin the apostle Paul ever is. His mind is always on Christ, and his glory, never brooding on the past. All we see in his epistles is a passing reference to it, in relation to other things, but no preoccupation with it.

Here, then, is a burden of depression through being unable to forgive oneself. If this is true of us, then we must be told roundly, in the Lord's name, that we are indulging in something that we simply cannot afford, and must stop it. We must accept the forgiveness of God, and allow him to say that it is behind us. And if he says it is behind us, we are sinning if we continue to preoccupy ourselves with it. The morbid indulgence of it is a luxury, a luxury of misery. "Wilt thou be made whole? Do you really want deliverance?" It is clear that our Lord's question is a highly relevant one.

One of the dangers in such situations is the desire

to succumb to the pressures, and to give in to them because of the sheer weariness of the continuing struggle, and the spiritual drowsiness and torpor that comes upon the spirit. It is an even greater battle to resist this and to fight for wakefulness and watchfulness. We are told how, when a man is struggling through extreme conditions of intense cold, there comes an overwhelming desire to lie down and sleep; and the feeling of euphoria that comes over him in such a situation makes him feel that the most wonderful and releasing thing of all would be just to give in and lie down. This is the point of danger for him, and it is so also in the spiritual life. The will must fight here with the greatest kind of fierceness, and refuse to give up and give in. This is what the will to be made whole means and involves. We really need to want this more than anything else in the world.

Another factor that can have a real bearing on the problems of depression and despondency is that there is often a very real temptation to rest in our background and heredity, and blame our disability on things that happened to us when we were children. It may, of course, be true that early years have left a mark upon us; it can hardly be doubted that the experiences of childhood often have a very traumatic effect on human life. But it is quite another thing to take refuge in this, and to reserve in our inmost heart the right to say that because this is how it was in our childhood, we are not to blame for our present disability, and therefore have no responsibility for it. A great deal of harm can be done by allowing people to clutch at this straw as an excuse for sinking into apathy and despair. We need to recognise that the human mind is very resilient, and that the grace of God can overcome and overrule in all these matters.

The classical instance of this is found in the book of Ruth, in the story of Boaz. This is an invaluable encouragement to people who have had difficult and unfortunate backrounds. Boaz was the son of a harlot, and it does not need much imagination to realise what a gigantic chip on his shoulder he could have had, and the resentments, the bitternesses, the grudge against society, that he could have carried with him through life. Psychiatists tell us that this is the kind of background that makes for problem lives which are characterised, sometimes by a mean and grasping spirit, sometimes by a shrunkenness of spirit that has no redeeming characteristics. But here is a man with such a background, whose end result was very different, for he appears as one of the most gracious, generous and gentlemanly people that we find anywhere in Scripture. And the explanation is that the the grace of God had broken into that heritage which might humanly speaking have given rise to all kinds of psychological maladjustment, crippling him emotionally, psychologically and even morally.

Sadly enough, there is ample evidence in pastoral work for believing that backgrounds of trouble and difficulty in the home do indeed leave marks and scars that time itself does not heal. But, lest we should be tempted to accept such a pattern as inevitable, God has recorded the story of Boaz for us in Scripture. This is in much need of being remembered today. The grace of God can heal lives that have been marked by backgrounds of this nature, and can turn lives that have, humanly speaking, everything against them, into lovely and beautiful things, and lift them to high levels of living. There is no background, no family inheritance or influence, over which the grace of God cannot prevail.

But it is a great temptation to succumb to the negative, even fatalistic, attitude and assume that because of our background the situation is irreversible. This is where Christ's question becomes so relevant: "Boaz, you who have an atrocious family history, do you really want to be made whole?"

Nor should we underestimate the many quirks and twists in the human mind and spirit. There is, for example, the desire, sometimes conscious and sometimes unconscious, to evade the unpalatable in life by escaping into despondency or even illness, as has already been pointed out. There are many unpalatable things in life, and we simply have to learn to come to terms with them in a responsible manner, whether it be problems and difficulties in the home or the family or at work, or the frustation of thwarted prospects or relationships, or even limitations in our abilities that we are reluctant or unable to recognise, or the shock realisation that we are not so important in the world as we are in our own estimation.

All these considerations, and many others, are potential causes of depression, and the temptation to give in and crumple may on occasion be very real. This is where one's will has to be engaged, and where there has to be a little courage to face unpalatable truths, and a willingness to forge ahead, to grit one's teeth and say, "All right, this is my situation, but I will not allow it to master me and demoralise me. I may be in an impossible situation, but there is a God, and if he leaves me in it, when he could as easily take me out of it, there must be some reason for this. Let me find the reason and let me address myself to the situation." If we do this then we have found a practical and effective alternative to despondency and despair. Our souls may dress themselves in their Sunday clothes, and walk with dignity and stature in the world.

What we have to ask ourselves - and it can be a very disconcerting and disturbing question - is, "Is this morass that we have fallen into an escape from something we are not willing to face, some unpalatable truth about ourselves?" What if the right attitude, and the real alternative, should be to battle through and to say, "If I am going to go down, I will go down fighting, not drooping?" Can we rise to that challenge? Tennyson's words at the close of his poem Ulysses underline the challenge very fitly:

One equal temper of heroic hearts,
Made weak by time and fate, but strong in will
To strive, to seek, to find, and not to yield.

It may be true for us to say that we are not the stuff of which heroes are made, but it is just as certain that there are many ordinary folk who in their long battling with pain and anguish and sorrow and the many burdens that life has laid upon them, have come up fighting with the light of battle in their eyes, and have demonstrated a truly heroic spirit that has been an inspiration and a challenge, not to say rebuke, to all who know them.

It may be that in all our thinking in this chapter we hear a faint voice breaking in upon us. We are hardly sure what it is saying, but as we listen we can hear it summoning us, and our wills, out of the incredibly complex labyrinth of our mind, where all the pressures are upon us. It is the voice of Jesus, seeking a point of contact with us, as he says, "Wilt thou be made whole?" In the story in John 5 he recalled the impotent man to a new possibility and a new hope. And it may be, for someone who reads these words, that this is what he is doing now, challenging and summoning the will to exercise itself and to fight.

Suffering, hard-pressed, cast-down believer,
Wilt thou be made whole?

12

PETER'S DENIAL

Luke 22:62: "Peter went out, and wept bitterly."

It may be thought, at first glance, that the story of the apostle Peter's life, as recorded in the New Testament, does not give much evidence of spiritual depression - and this is true of the greater part of that story. But there is one point in particular on which we can focus, namely, the period between the time that Jesus died on the cross and the time that the news came to him that Jesus had risen from the dead - a dark period indeed, when he was left alone with his awful sense of failure, having three times denied his Lord.

Let us consider the situation: Peter in the Judgment Hall of Caiaphas the High Priest was confronted by the servant maid's challenge, and three times he denied that he knew Jesus, finally with oaths and cursing. We are told that "the Lord turned and looked upon Peter". This look devastated him, and he went out and wept bitterly. That was the beginning of a time of great bleakness and desolation and darkness for him. For, from that point onwards till the moment Jesus breathed his last on the cross, there was no opportunity for Peter to make amends, to say that he was sorry, or to ask forgiveness from the Lord. What must Peter have felt after three o'clock that Good Friday afternoon, when Jesus had died, with the shame and grief and sorrow of his denial so unalterable now, with no possibility of redress or of recovering the situation by pleading for forgiveness? What must it have been like for him that night and all through the next day with such a burden upon him, in addition to the natural grief he felt at losing his beloved Master? Is it beyond our imagination to envisage the deep spiritual darkness and desolation that surely overwhelmed him utterly, in a despair that must have felt to him to be total and irreversible.

What are the lessons that we can learn from this tragic story? First of all, we may readily recognise that it is possible for an experience of this nature to happen to us. It is by no means uncommon - and this is encountered from time to time in pastoral work - among people who have known a similar sense of desolation, when there has been no opportunity left to them to make amends or ask forgiveness in the case of someone they have wronged, because death has intervened to make this impossible.

There are two separate issues to be distinguished here. It would be true to say that it is a very common thing in the experience of bereavement for people in their sorrow and grief to reproach themselves with not having cared more for their loved ones when ill, for not having done more for them when they feel now they could have done, and for a great sense of guilt to come upon them, bringing distress, desolation and darkness upon their spirits, to compound their grief. "If only I had done (this) or (that), if only...if only...if only." And so they reproach themselves, sometimes inconsolably.

What needs to be recognised, however, is that this is part of the grief and bereavement process. It is a very common occurrence. And so often it is the enemy of souls turning his knife in the wound of grief and hurting us when we are in distress, and it needs to be resisted and refused. One has known people whose care of their loved ones has been wonderful and moving to behold; they have not only done their duty by them, but far exceeded it, and done more than could ever have been expected of them, and yet they reproach themselves with the agonising thought 'if only...if only', taking upon themselves an enormous burden of guilt that bears no relation to reality. This is something that needs the tenderest and most gentle assurance and comfort, and wise pastoral ministry can do much to ease the burden and lead their distressed hearts into peace.

But there is also the real, as distinct from the imagined or exaggerated, feeling of guilt, when there truly has been neglect, or lack of compassion, or failure to do all that might have been done. There are indeed situations of estrangement, when the opportunity to say we are sorry was let slip, and it is no longer possible - because of hurt pride, or resentment, or bitterness and ill-will, or whatever - (with Peter it was cowardice and self-regard).

We must recognise, however, that for Peter it was rather different from what it can possibly be for us in one special respect: Peter was forgiven, and there was a special message of assurance from the risen Christ for him: "Go, tell the disciples, and Peter, that he is risen from the dead." But in the nature of the case, we cannot have that assurance from beyond death in that same way, for our loved ones do not rise from the dead in this world, and do not, and cannot, come back from the dead to give us that kind of assurance.

Still that does not mean that there is no hope for us, in such a situation, for there is forgiveness. We may seek and find forgiveness from God for what we have done, and there is time for amendment of life. We learn the hard way, but we may really learn. There is hope. It is possible quietly and lovingly to insist this to a mourning heart that has been grieving because of a failure to do all that might have been done to help a loved one in time of need and crisis and mortal illness. That forgiveness needs to be laid hold of; and God means that we should lay hold of it.

But - and this is something to be given full consideration - prevention is better than cure in such a situation. To understand what is meant by this statement it will be necessary to look at the history and the antecedents of Peter's terrible and tragic failure which led to his bleak and dark experience of despair.

On any estimate, Peter was a big man, a natural leader of men, big-hearted, and generous in spirit. And yet there were weaknesses, largely hidden from view, but presenting significant and fateful symptoms from time to time. Shakespeare makes the Queen say to Hamlet, in answer to his question about the 'play within the play', "The lady doth protest too much, methinks." It is very revealing to look at Peter's protestations in the Gospel record. On one occasion he said to Jesus, "Lord, I am ready to go with thee, though into prison, and to death" (Luke 22:33); on another he said, "Though I should die with thee, yet will I not deny thee" (Matt. 26:35); on yet another, in the Upper Room, he said, "Thou shalt never wash my feet" (John 13:8), thereby consciously or unconsciously implying his superiority to the other disciples. The question we have to ask is, "Who was he trying to convince? The others? Or Jesus? Or himself?" Perhaps a little of all three, but, we may suspect, especially himself.

Was he conscious of an inner uncertainty, then, within himself, which made him over-compensate in terms of bluster and such forthright - yes, 'boasting' is the word, for that is surely how it must have come over to the other disciples. This was the point that Jesus made in the resurrection encounter on the shores of Galilee, "Simon, son of Jonas, lovest thou me more than these?" as if to say, "What price now your protestations of greater love and loyalty than any of the others?"

There is a phrase we sometimes use today in describing a man - "he is whistling in the dark" - by which we mean that there is an underlying uncertainty and fear in him, and he is trying to reassure and cheer himself up by whistling. He is afraid of the dark, and this is how he deals with his fear. But there is a certain dishonesty in this; he is not facing up to how things really are with him, and that is why he is whistling in the dark.

There was surely something of this in Simon Peter, and it will be useful to consider him in this light for a little. His strong and marked reaction to our Lord's teaching about the Cross and the need for disciples to take up that Cross has often been noted. Why did Peter baulk at Jesus' teaching that he must die? It was because he saw the implications of this on his own life. The reason why he baulked at taking up the cross himself was that he was afraid of it because he was conscious of his weakness and the cowardice of his own heart.

There is a telling phrase in Galatians 2:12 about Peter's reaction in a particular situation, where we are told that "he withdrew and separated himself, fearing them which were of the circumcision (i.e. the Jews)." The circumstances were as follows: after the vision he received in Acts 10 about 'common or unclean' things, which signalled the admission of the Gentiles into the blessings of the gospel, Peter was prepared and happy to have table fellowship with Gentile believers; but when Jewish Christians came down from Jerusalem to Antioch he changed his tune, for fear of them. This was simply the articulation of 'fear of anything' that was deep down in his nature, and it is this that surfaced in the Judgment Hall. True, we are told in the story of the trial of Jesus that "Peter followed afar off," but we should not misunderstand this. It does not refer to Peter's keeping his distance, rather, it was an evidence of his impulsive nature - and his 'whistling in the dark', and his failure to come to terms with himself. All the other disciples had by this time forsaken Jesus and fled; Peter's attitude seems to have been, "I'll show them, I'm not afraid."

But he was afraid. And bluster is not the best way to deal with fear, for it is a failure to recognise one's weaknesses. It would have been far better for him to have admitted to himself that he was afraid, that he was a coward. Then things might have been different in the Judgment Hall, he might well have found himself taking a deep breath, so to speak, and saying, "Yes, I am one of his disciples," and facing the inevitable consequences of doing so. That would have been to recognise his own weakness and, recognising it, to lean not on the arm of the flesh as he did, but on the strength of the Lord alone. That is the basic difference between, as we sometimes say, 'keeping your chin up' and 'sticking your neck out'. So often it was the latter attitude rather than the former that characterised Peter, and it was, in the last analysis, because he was unsure of himself, with an unsureness that he never admitted to himself.

What Peter needed was to come to terms with himself, to face the truth about himself and, recognising his weakness, to cast himself on the enabling of the Lord. It was because he failed to do so that disaster finally overtook him in the Judgment Hall. This is why the post-resurrection encounter and confrontation on the shores of the Sea of Galilee must have been such a painful and devastating experience for him. On any estimate of this remarkable story, it is clear that our Lord meant that meeting to be an inquest on Peter's failure, as he countered Peter's threefold denial with his threefold challenge, "Simon, son of Jonas, lovest thou me?"

It can hardly be without significance that when the disciples came in to land after their abortive fishing expedition they saw a fire of coals on the shore prepared by Jesus. The only other occasion in which a fire of coals is mentioned in the Gospels is in the record of that fateful scene in the Judgment Hall when Peter denied his Lord (John 18:18). Jesus was deliberately reminding him of what had happened that night. True, he had sent a personal word to Peter after his resurrection - "Go, tell the disciples and Peter..." - as a token to the despairing disciple of the Divine forgiveness; but the problem of his wayward heart had not been dealt with, and now the time of reckoning had come, when he was obliged to face the truth about himself. And how penetrating were our Lord's dealings with him! Even in his tenderness and love he was devastatingly faithful, as he exposed the emptiness of Peter's blustering protestations of loyalty and love. It can hardly be doubted that Peter went from that interview with new insights into his own heart and a new self-perception, sorely chastened and humbled, but with a new realism about himself and a new determination about the future.

This is what was meant when we said earlier that prevention is better than cure. Peter's downfall was entirely predictable - indeed, Jesus himself predicted it - because of the kind of man he was, and because he had failed all along the line to know himself and to come to a realistic assessment of his own weaknesses and limitations. If he had been prepared to face the truth about himself and come to terms with it, his story might have read very differently.

Such a reappraisal, painful though it may be, is a possibility for any of us. It is included in the Divine purposes for all God's children, in conforming us to the image of his Son, that we should, in coming to an ever deepening knowledge of him, also come to a true knowledge of ourselves, and so come to a true wholeness and integrity of life.

13

LOW-SPIRITEDNESS

2 Timothy 1:7: "God hath not given us the spirit of fear; but of power, and of love, and of a sound mind."

One of the purposes in these studies in spiritual depression is to enable us to relate them to our own situation and our own experience. It is not so much that they should be portraits of us, as that rather we should be able to say, "There is something of that in me - something of David, or of Elijah under the juniper tree, or of Jonah" - and so apply the teaching of the Word as to get real help and encouragement in our situation.

This is the kind of lesson that we may learn from a study of what the New Testament tells us about Timothy, Paul's son in the faith; and just as important as the portrait of Timothy is the record of Paul's dealing with him. Indeed, this is one of the most valuable of studies, from the point of view of the pastoral counselling it affords.

The picture that is given us, both in Acts and in the Epistles, is of a young man of undoubted devotion and loyalty, faithful and honourable in the work of the gospel; and yet, despite this, he stands out clearly as a man who was timid by nature, not a little fearful, easily discouraged, and with a marked tendency to low-spiritedness. If we were to use modern, everyday expressions, we would not be far from the mark if we said that Timothy tended to be rather fragile, or, as we sometimes say, a little bit 'precious'. This is the Timothy of the New Testament. To be like this can, in certain circumstances, be a fairly fruitful cause of depression of spirit, - not, perhaps, the deep dark moods which characterised Elijah, when all he wanted was to die, but sufficiently significant to be a troublesome and indeed a distressing reality in the believer's experience - the kind of attitude that we sometimes describe as 'making heavy weather' of life.

Let us look first of all at some of the relevant passages:

In 2 Timothy 1:4, the words "being mindful of thy tears" are very revealing: not only do they show that Paul was deeply attached to Timothy, they also tell us something significant about Timothy's make-up, as one who could be easily discouraged.

In 1 Timothy 5:23, Paul's famous injunction to "drink no longer water, but use a little wine for thy stomach's sake" shows Timothy to have been not the most robust of people physically, and to have been often in ill-health and off-colour.

In 1 Corinthians 16:10, Paul's eloquent 'aside' serves to underline Timothy's natural timidity and fearfulness. One can imagine how much it must have cost him to have gone to Corinth into the midst of the difficulties and animosities that abounded in the Christian fellowship there. It is hardly surprising that Paul should have said, "See that he may be with you without fear."

In 1 Timothy 4:12, the well-known exhortation to "let no man despise thy youth" seems to suggest that on occasion Timothy tended to shrink from a proper assertion of his   rightful authority, and that he would do so because of his natural timidity of spirit.

In 2 Timothy 1:8, he is encouraged, perhaps against this fearful spirit, to face shame for Christ's sake, and in 2 Timothy 2:3 to endure hardness - perhaps the operative word being not so much 'hardness' as 'endure', as if to exhort him not to crumble under pressure.

These references provide   useful   and significant pointers as to the kind of person Paul's young colleague was, and they enable us to build up a picture of him.

There is an instinctive reaction in some, by nature hardier, spirits to such people, which makes them tend to dismiss them in an attitude bordering on contempt. But we need to look carefully at such a reaction, for not only does it represent a devastating emotional and psychological 'bludgeoning' which can do untold harm (how insensitive, even callous, we can sometimes be towards the 'lame ducks' of this world!), but also, more importantly, this was not Paul's way with Timothy, and it certainly is not the Lord's way with men. How much better it is to do as Paul did with Timothy, for in spite of his low-spiritedness he was a young man that the Apostle had enough confidence in to send on important and critical missions in the gospel (1 Thess. 3:2ff.).

This is perhaps a point at which we could usefully say that, even in the   context of problems and difficulties, Christians need not thereby be incapacitated for Christian service. The tendency, of course, in a state of low-spiritedness, is precisely to opt out of service. " What use can I be to anybody, what good can I do?" we say. The danger here of self-pity is very real, and this is where low-spiritedness can become a chronic condition, and plunge us into depression and quiet despair. But Paul refused to allow Timothy to sink into such a morass. With quiet insistence he drove this young man, and kept him at it. He knew just how far he could push Timothy; he was sufficiently a realist to know that there were some things that Timothy could not be pushed to do, but also that there were many that he could, and needed for his own good to be pushed to do. One is prompted to observe that this is good psychology, because to be allowed to lie down to this kind of stress is the one fatal thing.

This is why we find Timothy engaged in various tasks and assignments in the work of the gospel. In 2 Corinthians 1:19, for example, we see that he was present with Paul during his preaching at Corinth, and that on a later occasion he had been sent by the Apostle to Macedonia (Acts 19:21,22), and thence to Corinth (1 Cor. 4:17). Paul did not hesitate to send this low-spirited young man into the very lion's den, as it were, at Corinth, although he was clearly afraid that he might be timid (1 Cor. 16:11) and bespoke a good reception for him. There is also a reference in Philippians 2:19-23 to another mission that was entrusted to him.

Two things emerge from all this. One is Paul's undoubted regard and affection for his son in the faith, and his appreciation of all his good points and qualities; the other is the fact that a man with these undoubted weaknesses, and evident low-spiritedness, was challenged and encouraged, apparently successfully, to serve the Lord in the gospel, and was able to assume major responsibilities in its ongoing work.

W.E. Sangster, of Westminster, once made the comment that "Jesus sees double... He sees us not only as the people we are, but also as the people we might become." We all need something of this double vision about people, to enable us to see the best in them, for if we see what men can become, we shall persevere with them, and deal with them in a certain way. And it is far, far better to take calculated risks, and show confidence in such people, even though we sometimes may make mistakes, than to wash one's hands of them.

This is what Paul does with Timothy, as a wise pastor and counsellor. He is dealing with a young Christian who tends to be low-spirited, and has a gloominess and a fragility about him that makes heavy weather of life; and he refuses to let him sink down into apathy, but prods him and keeps on prodding him, and succeeds in getting him to snap out of it.

Let us look, then, at the situation to which Paul addresses himself in 2 Timothy. The Apostle is in prison, his days are numbered, he is soon to be offered up (4:6). There is no doubt at all that the times are difficult and that Timothy is under pressure. Nor does it need much imagination to realise the kind of fears and dreads that would be gripping this sensitive young man, and giving him these awful, panicky feelings within him and the sense of being overwhelmed. "What will I do if Paul is put to death?" he would doubtless think (it was fairly clear by this time that the Apostle was not going to be released). "What is to become of me?" We might be tempted to say that it was little wonder Timothy was making heavy weather and feeling extremely dispirited.

This is a point at which we can usefully ask, "Do we see ourselves reflected in this situation?" Are we making heavy weather with life, for whatever cause, whatever reason? Are we in a dreary dispirited condition and have we a dreary dispirited attitude to life? We need to see how Paul's pastor-heart deals with this situation. He devotes two entire epistles to the matter, writing words of exhortation and encouragement to Timothy. This is why there is so much robust and positive healthy teaching in what he writes to his son in the faith.

The nature of this teaching in both of the Pastoral Epistles, particularly the second, is twofold. On the one hand, there is an element of challenge and almost rebuke in what he says. Paul is dealing firmly and decisively, even if gently and lovingly, with Timothy, challenging his low-spiritedness, jolting him out of it, taking him to task about it as something that ought not to be. On the other hand, in the very challenge he makes, he shows the divine provision that is the abundant answer to such low-spiritedness.

We should note very carefully the words in 2 Timothy 1:11,12, "Whereunto I am appointed... for the which cause I suffer these things," and in 2:9, "Wherein I suffer trouble," the emphasis on Paul's own experience of suffering. We should not miss the significance of this, for the Apostle is not only holding up his own sufferings and his reaction to them as an example and encouragement to Timothy, but also - and this is a lesson of great importance for us - he is implying a very different reaction to sufferings and pressures from that shown by his young friend and colleague. And lest Timothy - and the Timothys of this world - might be tempted to say, "It is all very well for Paul to be impatient of our fears and tremblings, he is strong, and does not have our fragile temperament and make-up," the point must be made very clearly and firmly that Paul's temperament and make-up were not so very different from Timothy's. Indeed they were very similar.

Paul was, naturally, of a timorous and fearful temperament. When he wrote to the Corinthians, he said, "I was with you in weakness, and in fear, and in much trembling" (1 Cor. 2:3). Later, writing to these same Corinthians he wrote, "Without were fightings, within were fears" (2 Cor. 7:5). On two or three occasions God appeared to him in vision, saying, "Fear not". But what Paul did with these fears and timidities and tendencies to low-spiritedness was to battle with them and overcome them. "Most gladly, therefore, will I glory in my infirmities... for when I am weak, then am I strong" (2 Cor. 12:9,10).

It is all a question of having a right attitude to our recognised weaknesses and fragilities, and to have spirit enough to wrestle with them, refusing to give in to them, wresting promises from God in the darknesses we face.

This can be definitive for all the rest of life; but not to wrestle means that secretly, unconsciously, or even perhaps openly, we shall excuse ourselves from the disciplines of battle, and therefore make excuses for ourselves, and make allowances for the fragilities which ought to be nailed and crucified. And we shall remain fragile and precious, and shall always make heavy weather; we shall remain people who give in far too easily to circumstances. We shall remain morally and spiritually flabby.

Paul accordingly challenges the young Timothy to take himself in hand. It is in this context that he exhorts him to "stir up the gift of God" that is in him. This is a significant phrase. The 'gift' referred to has to do with the divine enduement bestowed on Timothy in his ordination by the Apostle. The word 'stir' here means 'to kindle' or 'to stir up into flame', and would be the word used to describe the action of breaking up a fire that had been banked up and left with the air vent closed for some time. It is the first thing that we do when we come in out of the cold on a winter's night - we take the poker and stir up the fire to let the air in, and presently the flames are leaping up and a cheery warmth is being diffused throughout the room. The fire was not out, but it was not getting air, and it was not giving heat; it needed disturbing in order to make it fulfil its true function.

In the same way, the fire that has been implanted in us can never go out, but from time to time it needs to be disturbed and stirred into flame.

But how does one stir into flame the spiritual life? According to Paul, it is by the exercise of the mind. In 1 Timothy 4:15 he says, "Meditate upon these things; give thyself wholly to them." This is the only effectual way: when the knowledge of what we are in Christ, and what God has made us in him, is quiescent in us, we really need to do some hard thinking in order that the sheer wonder and glory of it might grip us afresh. It cannot be too firmly insisted that there is no other adequate and proper way of doing it than this. It cannot be done by mere psychological methods as, for example, by stirring up the emotions. It must begin in the mind. One of our hymns says,

Think what Spirit dwells within thee,
What a Father's smile is thine,

What thy Saviour died to win thee:
Child of heaven, shouldst thou repine?"

That is the point: if we really think on these things, and think them through, they will take a grip on us, and the repining and the low-spiritedness will be dealt with. The pressures will remain: thinking about God's grace in Christ will not remove the pressures, but it will most certainly deal with our attitudes to them. And it is when our minds are gripped by the glories of grace that the fires begin to burn afresh in the soul.

But we must look more particularly at what Paul says in the remarkable 7th verse of the chapter, where he sets in contrast 'the spirit of fear' (which Timothy is tending to show) and 'the spirit of power, and of love, and of a sound mind'. First of all, we may recognise that, since the spirit of fear is something God has not given us, then to display it, and to be gripped by it, is a denial of our calling in Christ. The word 'fear' is better translated 'cowardice', and has its root in the notion of 'shrinking', and it is over against this that the Divine gift (mentioned in the previous verse as requiring to be stirred up) is set, namely the wealth of what we have and are in Christ, described now as 'the spirit of power, and of love, and of a sound mind'. The words 'sound mind' translate a Greek word which in its verbal form means 'to be in one's senses', or 'in one's right mind', and what it suggests is this: 'to be in one's right mind' in the Christian sense is to be what we are in Christ, and to be this means that the natural timorousness within us is displaced and discounted.

Furthermore, it is this 'being in one's right senses' that conditions the other two qualities of power and love.

This is an important consideration, for the one without the other - power without love, or love without power - means imbalance and distortion. As W. Lock, in his I.C.C. Commentary points out, "The Christian minister must be strong, efficient, courageous, but never forget personal tenderness for others....." And when Christ - or one of Christ's true men - takes us in hand, dealing in grace with us, there is that marvellous combination of power and love - tenderness, compassion, understanding of our weakness and need, our battles, our failures, yet never any suggestion of condoning them, but rather spurring us to new endeavour. This is the 'right mind' and 'being squared with oneself, coming to terms with oneself', which is the point of Paul's exercise here.

Two contrasting attitudes unfolded in the Scriptures may be taken to make this point: the experience of the patriarch Jacob in the Old Testament, and that of the apostle Paul in the New. In the marvellous story in Genesis we are told how, when Jacob's sons returned from Egypt and reported Joseph's stipulation that young Benjamin should return with them when they next visited Egypt for supplies of corn, he cried in distress and dejection of spirit, "All these things are against me... My son shall not go down with you, for his brother is dead, and he is left alone: if mischief befall him by the way in which ye go, then shall ye bring down my gray hairs with sorrow to the grave" (42:36-38). Jacob, it is true, was by this time an old man, but his attitude is eloquent of the dispiritedness which characterised his later life. This is one attitude to life in its difficulties and pressures: it was Timothy's attitude.

Paul's attitude, however, stands in complete contrast. Here is a man who knew that within a very short time he was to be martyred for Christ's sake. And this is how he speaks:

God hath saved us, and called us with an holy calling, not according to our works, but according to his own purpose and grace, which was given us in Christ Jesus before the world began, but is now made manifest by the appearing of our Saviour Jesus Christ, who hath abolished death, and hath brought life and immortality to light through the gospel: Whereunto I am appointed a preacher, and an apostle, and a teacher of the Gentiles. For the which cause I also suffer these things: nevertheless I am not ashamed: for I know whom I have believed, and am persuaded that he is able to keep that which I have committed unto him against that day (2 Timothy 1:9-12).

Here, then, are the two attitudes: "All these things are against me," and "All things work together for good to them that love God." And it is open to us to choose which is to be our attitude to the 'slings and arrows of outrageous fortune'. We can be fragile, we can be low-spirited - or we can get the bit between our teeth and be like the apostle Paul. We may choose to be true to our spiritual nature and our spiritual inheritance. If God has given us, not a spirit of fear, but a spirit of power, as indeed he has in Christ, it does not matter what we are by temperament and by nature, it does not matter how timid or how fragile we are, or how much the tendency to low-spiritedness is within us, the overwhelming reality of what we are in him offsets and displaces every natural and human consideration to make us more than conquerors.

This is the perspective to which Paul calls the young Timothy in the verses just quoted. The way, he means, to be "partaker of the afflictions of the gospel according to the power of God" is to remember the greatness of the gospel that has saved us (2 Timothy 1:9ff).

On the one hand, he speaks of our calling, rooted in eternity, planned from the beginning, before all worlds. The sovereign electing grace, which all through life has brooded over us, long before it ever appeared likely that we should be saved - this is the grace that is near at hand to bless when we are called to bear our witness to Christ. Does not this give us strength and encouragement, to know that from all eternity such suffering has been in the Divine plan for us, and that it has its integral place in the fulfilment of God's purposes of redemption (cf. 1 Peter 5:10) - should not this be sufficient to undergird our faltering spirits, and enable us to hold up our heads?

On the other hand, he reminds Timothy, and us, that predestination and election are not metaphysical concepts unrelated to anything except the realm of thought, but have an historical locus, in the incarnation of the Son of God, and come into focus in history. They are worked out, and fulfilled, in his coming and appearing on earth, by which he has abolished death and brought life and immortality to light through the gospel. And to meditate on this, to allow ourselves to be gripped and mastered by the grandeur and the glory of such a concept - this is surely the antidote to low-spiritedness and fearfulness.

14

DOUBTING CASTLE

1 John 5:13: "....that ye may know that ye have eternal life."

The words which form the title of our next study are taken from John Bunyan's *Pilgrim's Progress,* in a section of the book that tells how the pilgrims Christian and Hopeful strayed into Bypath Meadow, and found themselves in Doubting Castle as prisoners of Giant Despair. One cannot but be impressed by the deep spiritual insights that Bunyan had into the experiences of God's people, and the phrase 'Doubting Castle' is a graphic and evocative one, not only speaking of doubts, but of being shut up in a dark prison from which there seems to be no escape, with all efforts to do so doomed to failure. Those who have been in such a situation will know just how distressing and despair-making the experience of doubt can be.

There is a notable chapter in the Westminster Confession of Faith, entitled 'Assurance of Grace and Salvation', which reads as follows:

Although hypocrites, and other unregenerate men,

148

may vainly deceive themselves with false hopes and carnal presumptions of being in the favour of God and estate of salvation; which hope of theirs shall perish; yet such as truly believe in the Lord Jesus, and love him in sincerity, endeavouring to walk in all good conscience before him, may in this life be certainly assured that they are in the state of grace, and may rejoice in the hope of the glory of God; which hope shall never make them ashamed.

This certainty is not a bare conjectural and probable persuasion, grounded upon a fallible hope; but an infallible assurance of faith, founded upon the divine truth of the promises of salvation, the inward evidence of those graces unto which these promises are made, the testimony of the Spirit of adoption witnessing with our spirits that we are the children of God, which Spirit is the earnest of our inheritance, whereby we are sealed to the day of redemption.

No-one who reads these words could fail to realise the thoroughness with which the Westminster divines dealt with the great basic truths of our salvation; and there is nothing that can strengthen our assurance of grace and salvation more powerfully and effectively than simply to steep ourselves in the deep truths of the Divine revelation in Jesus Christ. It would not be too much to say that a great many of the doubts and much of the lack of assurance that are productive of despondency and depression of spirit flow from a defective understanding of the meaning of salvation, and that the primary need is for a true and solid foundation for faith. It is true, of course, that initial doubts about salvation are quite common - they are part of the 'teething troubles' of new spiritual life, and they generally give way to a settled peace, as a proper understanding of the issues of salvation comes home to their heart. But sometimes, the doubts do not subside, and sometimes also, after a period of spiritual balance and activity, doubts can return to distress and dismay the hearts of God's people. What are we to say about such a situation?

We may put it thus (to take an analogy from the medical sphere). The medical profession recognises that a great deal of care needs to be given in the birth of a baby, and that a great deal depends upon proper skill and technique in both ante-natal and post-natal care, as well as at the birth itself, if the baby is going to be given a proper chance in life. It is so also in the spiritual realm. The apostle Peter speaks of salvation in terms of being born again of the incorruptible seed of the Word of God; and if there is carelessness or ignorance, if there is the application of wrong principles or wrong practice, it is very likely that harm will come to a babe in Christ.

Bringing souls to the birth in Christ is a critical matter, and if it is trivialized through carelessness or over-simplistic thinking all sorts of complications are likely to develop. And this, in fact, is what often happens. It is not unknown, for example, for spiritual birth to be forced and premature. People can be pressurised into making decisions for Christ before they are ready, before they are willing to come to him; and even when, in such circumstances, a genuine spiritual birth takes place, that spiritual life will, in all probability, have a whole crop of problems and difficulties that would not otherwise have occurred, if the birth had been more carefully nursed.

It is only too possible for a defective evangelism to be practised in which emotional pressures and the creation of atmosphere are made to do duty as spiritual work, instead of a worthy presentation of the truth of God by which alone a living faith can be born; and when emotions are stirred and deeply moved to a commitment to Christ without any clear or rational understanding of what is involved in the gospel, trouble is sure to result. When the emotion subsides, as it will, doubts will be sure to come crowding in, because a true basis for faith has never really been established.

One cannot but be impressed by the contrast to this that the words of the Shorter Catechism represent, in its statements about justification and faith:

> Justification is an act of God's free grace, wherein he pardoneth all our sins, and accepteth us as righteous in his sight, only for the righteousness of Christ imputed to us and received by faith alone.

> Faith in Jesus Christ is a saving grace, whereby we receive and rest upon him alone for salvation, as he is offered to us in the gospel.

Not a single word in either of these statements is superfluous, and they serve to encapsulate the central issues of salvation as given us in the Scriptures.

Here, then, is one real answer to the problem of doubts and lack of assurance, and the depression that comes through them. We must wrestle with the great truths of salvation, think them through, and work at them until they grip and master us.

Jesus, thy blood and righteousness
My beauty are, my glorious dress:
Midst flaming worlds, in these arrayed,
With joy shall I lift up my head.

Bold shall I stand in that great day;
For who ought to my charge shall lay?
Fully absolved through these I am
From sin and fear, from guilt and shame.

Zinzendorf's majestic words in this great hymn go to the root of the matter. A man who understands the meaning of these profound statements and gets into the heart of what they say is a man who is well on the way to solving the problems of assurance and doubt, and his heart will glow with the glory of the gospel.

Another consideration, akin to what has just been said and connected with it - and a significant contributory factor in the incidence of low-spiritedness - is the lack of any proper appreciation of the wonder and glory of salvation, and of the sheer joy of knowing the Saviour's love in the experience of it. It is only too evident that there are many believers who seem to know little of the sheer marvel and mystery and sweetness of the love of God in Christ, such as is evident in the words of the old hymn:

I stand all amazed at the love Jesus offers me,
Confused at the grace that so fully he proffers me;
I tremble to know that for me he was crucified,
That for me, a sinner, he suffered, he bled and died.

I marvel that he would descend from his throne divine,
To rescue a soul so rebellious and proud as mine;
That he should extend his great love unto such as I,
Sufficient to own, to redeem and to justify.

O it is wonderful that he should care for me enough to die for me!
O it is wonderful, wonderful to me!

These are the words of a man moved to the depths of his being by the consciousness and realisation of the Divine love. It is not emotionalism that makes a man speak thus, but rather an appreciation of the wonder and glory of a great salvation, and a grasp with mind and heart of the message of God's love in Christ. When a man gets to that point in his spiritual life, he knows the meaning of Paul's words, "joy and peace in believing." And when we can speak in this way from our hearts, spiritual despondency is likely to be foreign to our experience.

There is a lesson here for low-spiritedness and depression in general. What is often needed in our spiritual lives is a renewed awareness of the Divine love to dawn upon our souls. We must be more like the Psalmist when he said, "While I was musing the fire burned" (Ps. 39:3). The story is told of the American evangelist D.L. Moody who once, in the midst of his busy evangelistic outreach, became conscious of a certain coldness of heart and staleness in his work. He felt he could not allow this to go on, so he took time off to examine afresh the evidences in the New Testament of the love of Christ; and in a few days he returned to his work, with a broken heart, and a renewed vision, and on fire for God!

Our next consideration must be the doubts and lack of assurance that can spring from problems of natural temperament.

We sometimes speak of 'doubting Thomases', a term deriving from the experience of the disciple of that name who clearly had a decidedly gloomy side to his nature that made him prone to look on the dark side of life. Sometimes the doubts that such people experience can reach an almost pathological level, and in extreme form can lead to the terrible situation in which the believer may come to the conclusion that he has committed some unpardonable and unforgiveable sin, and that there can be no hope of salvation for him. No one who has not been in such a position can possibly understand the agony and despair that this can bring to the human spirit. This is an extremely distressing pastoral problem, and one that merits careful and detailed discussion.

It may well be that when such a stage is reached there is a medical and clinical condition to be dealt with, but inasmuch and insofar as there is a spiritual element in the problem, two things may be said. The first is this: John Bunyan gets to the heart of the issue in *Pilgrim's Progress,* when he tells how Christian and Hopeful, being bludgeoned by Giant Despair in Doubting Castle and losing all hope of ever getting out, suddenly remembered that they possessed a key called Promise, which could open any door. And this key turned the lock of their prison cell and also the great door of the Castle and its outer gates, and they made their escape. Bunyan is saying that the promises of God are the key to the darkest of human experiences. One of our forbears in the Scottish Kirk coined the wonderful phrase, 'Trusting in the bare word of a promising God'. This means trusting in the face of everything in our experience that makes us feel that it cannot be so. This is what the Scripture enjoins us to do, and what our hymnwriters express so graphically:

When we in darkness walk,
Nor feel the heavenly flame,
Then is the time to trust our God,
And rest upon his Name.

Soon shall our doubts and fears
Subside at his control;
His loving-kindness shall break through
The midnight of the soul.

The second thing relates to what has already been said. It is a matter of trusting in spite of everything - even, as the Apostle John says, "if our heart condemn us" (1 John 3:20), for God is greater than our heart. This does not, of course, mean that we are to fly in the face of conscience, and that is not what John is speaking of; rather, we may be utterly convinced that we are not in a state of grace, with all the attendant distress, pain and anguish that that brings to us, and still be mistaken about the reality of the situation. For our heart, in such circumstances, is not the most reliable of guides; and God's promise stands over against all the undoubted feelings of abandonment and the sense of rejection and despair we may have, to proclaim to us his unchanging love and grace. The Psalmist once cried, in his distress, "No man cared for my soul" (Ps. 142:4) - this was the verdict and conviction of his heart, but he was wrong; in the ultimate sense it is never true, for God's love and care are never so near as when our hearts tell us we are utterly forsaken. God is greater than our hearts; and as we continue to lean on his promises, there comes at last the wonderful assurance that he will bring us into a large place.

But, to speak more specifically about what is sometimes called 'the unpardonable sin,' there is a need to establish quite clearly what is meant in Scripture by this term, as used by our Lord himself, in Matthew 12:31,32.

There are those, for example, who identify a particular sin which they have committed as being so terrible as to be unpardonable; and their problem is solved when they are assured that what they have done can indeed be pardoned and forgiven by a loving God. Sometimes people have brooded on some secret sin or enslaving habit about which they feel so terribly that they think God cannot possibly forgive them - something in their past, of which they are deeply ashamed, or some blasphemy they have spoken or thought. But they need to be assured, on the authority of God's Word, that this is not the unpardonable sin, and that it can be forgiven, however heinous it may be in their eyes. "Though your sins be as scarlet," says the Lord, "they shall be as white as snow" (Isaiah 1:18).

There are others who are unable to pinpoint any particular sin, but simply have the consciousness that since they do not seem to be able to find peace and assurance they must have committed something unpardonable, and there is therefore no hope for them. Others still, beset it may be with evil and impure thoughts and blasphemies, darting into their minds, may feel that they have yielded to the awful suggestions at some point, and taken a blasphemy upon their lips or in their hearts against the Spirit of God, and they conclude that there is no hope for them, and they are plunged into the deepest despair.

There are some things to be said about this. By definition, this sin against the Holy Spirit, since it is unforgivable, is not a sin that a true believer can ever commit; for a true believer is a forgiven person. Further, it is not a specific or particular sin, so much as an attitude. Ultimately, it can only be the sin of continuing and persistent refusal of the Spirit's grace, a hardness, and a hardened state of heart brought about by continued, deliberate and wilful rebellion against God and the pleadings of his Spirit.

This may be elaborated by pointing out that there are two constituent elements in all sin, the human, wayward element and the 'spiritual' and essentially evil element. This twofold combination is well expressed in Isaiah 53:6 in the words, 'All we like sheep have gone astray, we have turned every one to his own way.' In the first part of the verse we have the human, wayward element, that calls forth the compassion of Christ; in the second the deliberate and rebellious element. Every sin combines these two in some proportion; and the more the rebellious and deliberate preponderates over the wayward, the more dangerous and demonic the sin becomes, until it loses all its wayward element and becomes utterly wilful, finally passing the point of no return (this is why pride is much more dangerous than immorality, because immorality stems from the weakness and waywardness of the human heart, whereas pride is essentially evil, the direct spawn of the devil in the human soul).

This is the sin unto death of which the apostle John speaks (1 John 5:16), for which there is no pardon. It is the nature of sin that it imperceptibly passes from the one aspect to the other. Peter's denial may be taken as a case in point: his first act of denial was almost involuntary, due to the weakness of his nature; but in the second and third instances there was more than the wayward and the cowardly. There was something calculated and deliberate. The second and third times that we do things are always more wilful than the first. It is of the nature of sin that it should be so.

We see a solemn illustration of this hardening process in the story of King Herod. First of all he was interested in John the Baptist's preaching, an interest that developed into a conviction of sin as he listened to that fiery, turbulent messenger of God, and he became deeply disturbed by the Holy Spirit of God. At that point there was surely hope for his soul, wicked and evil and debauched though he was. But in that 'valley of decision' he resisted the Spirit's pleadings, and continued to resist until finally the Spirit was quenched, and left him. And the day came when, in the presence of Jesus, at the time of the trial, the Son of God had nothing to say to Herod, because he had passed the point of no return. He had sinned against the Holy Ghost; continued impenitence had hardened his heart beyond remedy. That is the sin for which there is no forgiveness.

But - and this is a very important consideration for our discussion - Herod was not worried in the least at that point, he was making fun and sport of Christ, and there was no spiritual burden on his soul, or fear of being in eternal danger. The man who has committed the unpardonable sin is not in any way concerned that he has done so; he is impervious to spiritual concern. By the same token, those who torment themselves with the terrifying fear of having committed that sin are by that very concern the most unlikely to have done so.

If it should be asked why some people should suffer in this distressing way, the answer would have to be that there is both a psychological and a spiritual basis to the problem. With many Christians, there seems to be an almost constitutional inability to believe the position God has given them in the adoption of sons, and therefore just to believe that they are really children of a loving Father, who looks on them with a fatherly care, tenderness and love. Instead they have a deeply intrenched conception of God as a rather stern, forbidding, almost tyrant-like figure, standing over them threateningly, ready to criticise or condemn their slightest deviation from the standards he has set them. In this regard, one wonders whether our Lord was drawing attention to such an attitude in the parable of the talents (Matt. 25:14-30). One has only to look at what the third servant in the parable said, "Lord, I knew thee that thou art an hard man... and I was afraid..." to see the point.

This is the crux of the matter. There is no evidence in the parable that his lord was *hard;* the other servants in the story did not react in this way. We are obliged to conclude that the problem with this servant was that he had a totally wrong conception of the lord in whose service he was engaged. *He had got it all wrong!* The evidence of the rest of the parable makes this clear.

Nor should we be slow to see what this wrong attitude did to him: it paralysed him as to any service he might have rendered; and the paralysis lasted for a lifetime. All through life, he was gripped and conditioned by this wrong attitude towards the lord he served. And this is the measure of how serious the issue can be in Christian life.

It may well be that this is caused at least in some measure by the psychological disability of an unhappy family background. Parents are in the place of God to their children in the first instance, and children get their first, instinctive ideas of what God is like from them. If the parent has been harsh, arbitrary, demanding, tyrannical, it is hardly surprising that this kind of 'picture' of God should be imposed upon a young mind, perhaps permanently, making belief in a loving God very uphill work.

And it is precisely when Christians have the concept of a capricious and arbitrary God rooted in their psychological makeup that they will find it difficult to believe that he can forgive them as he forgives other people. It is possible to turn such people to passages in the Scriptures that show very clearly that if we confess our sins God is faithful and just to forgive our sins, yet they will say, albeit unconsciously, that this applies to everybody else in the world, but for them it cannot apply. Their God is arbitrary and capricious, and unreasonable in the matter of forgiveness. This is a feeling more than a reasoned consideration, but it can sometimes be quite overpowering and devastating in its intensity.

The real and effectual answer to this distressing condition is that we should learn to believe in the tenderness of the Divine love, and to let that love bathe our wounds and our hurts until they are healed; to believe the love that God has for us, to see that love in the face of Jesus, and to know it is the most trustworthy and reliable reality in all the universe. We so readily forget the words, "Like as a father pitieth his children..." and "Your heavenly Father knoweth..." - knows when we are sunk in despondency and despair, engulfed by the awful darkness and anguish that such a condition brings. But it is so often then that he comes to us with messages of grace and love, eager to prove to us in our heartsore experience the reality of his boundless compassion and pity, and to lift us into the warmth and assurance of his love and care.

15

THE NEED FOR BALANCE

Ecclesiastes 3:1: "To every thing there is a season, and a time to every purpose under the heaven."

The well-known words in the third chapter of Ecclesiastes, with the remarkable and graphic portrayal of the times and seasons in the life of man, provide us with the title and theme of our next study. What is in view is the need for balance in spiritual life. In dealing with such a theme some care is needed, since what is to be said could well be open to misunderstanding and misconstruction. This, however, is a risk that will need to be taken, since the subject is an important one, and when neglected can be a fruitful source of spiritual depression and despondency.

By way of introduction, let us consider the following: on occasion, when a Christian gives a public testimony on how God has brought him to a knowledge of salvation, we may react with misgiving and a feeling of dismay and concern in our hearts, saying, "I have never had an experience like that; there must be something wrong with my spiritual life," and we go away feeling inadequate, a 'second-class' Christian, with something far wrong with us.

It would perhaps surprise us to know how common this experience is. It is not that that another Christian has deliberately or consciously suggested that we are on a lower spiritual plane, or that he is on a higher one (although sometimes this may be the case), but it is certainly the inference we may draw from it. It leads us into distress and despondency, and it may set in train a whole pattern of endeavour in us to induce or create something approximating to the experience described. This can lead to all sorts of spiritual problems and confusion.

Yet the truth of the matter is that dramatic, even spectacular, conversions are not necessarily the norm in Christian experience; and we have to balance stories of the dramatic with accounts in Scripture itself, as also in the history of the Church and in Christian experience, of a very different hue. There is the story of the conversion of Saul of Tarsus on the Damascus Road, it is true, and of the Philippian jailor's spectacular experience in the middle of the night; but there is also the story of Lydia (Acts 16:14), of whom it is said the Lord opened her heart, where the clear implication of the story - and the words used - is that her conversion was a gradual, unostentatious and quiet experience, unattended by any spectacular manifestation.

The problem here, then, is an imbalance in the understanding of the teaching of Scripture, which emphasises the immense variety of religious experience. What is often not grasped is that although a dramatic conversion from evil ways is, of course, an impressive testimony, it is surely better never to have been so low as to need a dramatic deliverance from darkness into light. We do not mean by this that people who do not sink low are not in such need of grace as those who do; rather, it is that although all men equally need grace, it remains true that some sins do not lend themselves to such dramatic deliverances as do others. Drunkenness and immorality and drug addiction are very glaring and obvious and deliverance from them can be dramatic in a way that deliverance from pride, envy or selfishness might not be.

This example, from a particular area of experience, may only be the tip of the iceberg, so to speak, but it illustrates in a graphic way an imbalance that can often do a great deal of harm and cause a great deal of distress and despondency for a believer, and it is highly desirable to try to disabuse despondent Christians of such mistaken thinking. One is prompted to comment in passing that this is where another of the great values of continuous and systematic exposition of the Scriptures can be seen, for Scripture does give a balanced view of these matters.

Another considerable source of despondency, not un-related to what has been said, lies in the problem that arises in our hearts when we read the accounts of the great inner conflict and distress said to be the mark of a genuine work of the Holy Spirit leading to conversion. One reads in notable biographies of great men of the faith and in accounts of spiritual awakening of experiences of this nature occurring; and it perplexes Christians and disturbs them greatly that they have not themselves had such experiences. All this leads to doubt and distress and despondency of spirit.

It is true that, as the Westminster Confession of Faith says, there may be much inward conflict, with many difficulties, before the believer reaches assurance of salvation, but we should not miss the significance of the word 'may' in the statement it makes. Such conflict is not a *sine qua non* of a true experience of grace, and genuine and authentic conversion to Christ can take place without it. Scripture nowhere insists that we must pass through a prolonged inner conflict before we can be converted. The writer recalls speaking with a young girl who became a Christian in her schooldays, and who when at university spoke of her concern at not having felt any conviction of sin in her experience until long after she embraced the offer of salvation. She was very perturbed about this, and wondered whether in view of this her profession of conversion was genuine and authentic. Yet she has been one of the loveliest and most consistent of Christians, serving for many years with great dedication on the mission field, with the beauty of the Lord our God resting upon her.

There are dangers here also, for it is possible, and it is often a real temptation, to try to induce such conflict in order to authenticate one's experience. In times of spiritual awakening, for example, there have been many evidences of deep distress and conflict due to conviction of sin, with ministers and elders roused from their sleep during the hours of the night to deal with anxious and seeking souls. These are authentic manifestations, whose validity need not be questioned. But it is another matter when earnest and zealous young people, well-meaning but less than wise, having pressed the gospel on their companions, wearing them down psychologically, and inducing in them a spurious willingness to come to Christ, produce a similar pattern to order, consciously or otherwise influenced by what they have heard and read about past awakenings, and desirous of seeing the same workings of the Spirit as in former days. Such pressurised experiences do not come to much and are responsible for many problems later.

The writer recalls a distressing experience in which a young girl, who had been greatly moved by the account of the public confession of sin that was such a marked characteristic of the Ruanda revival in East Africa, started a round of 'confession' in her church prayer meeting which spread rapidly in a highly charged emotional atmosphere. But it became increasingly clear as the meeting progressed that an alien spirit was at work, unhealthy and indeed abortive, for it led to precisely nothing. It proved to be a counterfeit manifestation. The thinking behind it, not conscious or deliberate, but nevertheless evident, was that since in the Ruanda revival confession of sin was a prominent feature therefore confession of sin would produce revival. This was the fallacy at work: it was the presence of the Spirit of God that produced confession in the Ruanda revival, but confession of sin does not 'produce' the Holy Spirit. What had in fact taken place was an unconscious attempt to induce revival. When this happens, and the attempts prove abortive, it raises all sorts of problems, and can lead to serious despondency and depression in those who are at a loss to know what has gone wrong. This is where an overview of Scripture can be of such immense value, since it enables us to discern the true from the false, and the wise from the unwise. This is what we mean when we speak of a question of balance.

There is need for a sense of balance in the doctrinal realm also. It is only too possible for there to be an over-emphasis on the more sombre aspects of the Christian faith, and when this occurs there is considerable likelihood that those who are the victims of it will become depressed. In a very perceptive and helpful article in the Free Church Monthly Record, Professor Donald MacLeod makes this point very well. He writes,

> That we have tended to over-emphasise the more sombre aspects of Christianity is probably true. This is not to deny these aspects: life is short, death is certain, judgement is imminent and hell is certain for the impenitent. It is a question of biblical proportion. These are not the major pre-occupations of Scripture. They are not even distinctively Christian. Yet some preachers seem to equate faithfulness with the constant reiteration of these truths; and even to regard the preaching of them as the only way to evangelise. In fact they are not evangelism at all. Evangelism is good news. More emphasis on the consecutive exposition of the scriptures would have preserved us from this imbalance and shut us in to giving proper biblical emphasis to the joyful, inspirational aspects of Christian truth.

It is all too easy for the mesage of doom to become a pathological condition in a man, which betrays a sickness of which he is quite unconscious. He is flying a distress signal without knowing it.

There is also a danger of imbalance in the realm of introspection. Looking inward, and examining oneself, is a necessary and a truly biblical exercise.

But something that is good in itself can become danger-ously perverted and unhealthy. It is all too possible to become morbidly preoccupied with one's inward states. Michael Griffiths, the former General Director of the Overseas Missionary Fellowship, commenting on student work in the Antipodes following a visit there, expressed concern that so much of it seemed to be "man-centred and problem-orientated, instead of being God-centred and goal-orientated." It is sadly true that many Christian lives seem to be 'problem- orien-tated', and it is not surprising that we have coined a word to describe this. 'Problem-itis' is a major difficulty in the Christian Church. It is not the fact that Christians have problems, but rather that they often tend to become morbidly preoccupied and obsessed with them, that can lead to despondency and depression.

One recalls the comment once made by a missionary leader who had had a particularly difficult and stress-ful time dealing with problems among missionary personnel. Speaking, in contrast, of three dedicated mis-sionaries he said, "Here are three good, solid girls of Presbyterian farming stock, who get their heads down and get on with the work. Give me people like that, for this is real missionary material." It was not that these girls did not have problems, but they were not preoccu-pied with them, and they had a sense of perspective, given them by their background and heritage, which enabled them to see that although there is a place for introspection, it does not have a principal place in the Christian's life.

One cannot but be impressed, in this connection, to realise how little the apostle Paul was preoccupied with looking inward. It is true, he confessed that he was less than the least of all the saints, and indeed chief of sinners, but a true assessment of his writings makes it abundantly clear that he was little preoccupied with his sins. No endless beatings of the breast with him! It disturbs not a little to find some of the seventeenth and eighteenth century divines in Scotland and England showing a more substantial preoccupation with the sinfulness of sin than with the good news of the gospel that deals with it. One recalls the statement made about them by a good modern-day Calvinist, 'They do get too preoccupied with their sins. You do not find that attitude in Calvin.' Those who know Calvin well will realise that such a statement could hardly be controverted.

It is all, of course, a matter of balance; and where there is imbalance one way or the other, a breeding ground for despondency and depression is inevitably prepared. To become over-preoccupied with one's problems is not a healthy state to be in; it is a recipe for all manner of problems and difficulties in spiritual life.

What are we to say, for example, about the young theological student who suddenly 'goes overboard' in involvement with the charismatic movement, claiming and exercising, as he sees it, all the gifts of the Spirit and seeking to proselytise all his companions in a manner that made one of them ask, only half jocularly, whether he had received the gift of humility; and a month or two later goes similarly 'overboard' in an extreme swing to Puritanism? The likelihood is that he was neither a genuine charismatic nor a genuine Puritan; rather, the extraordinary swings of the pendulum were evidences of a clutching at something to give him anchorage and security in his desperately uncertain state. He was flying distress signals, did he but know it, as the basic imbalance of his experience made clear.

Another problem area in Christian experience lies in the relation of the Christian Faith to culture. Down the centuries there has, of course, been an uneasy relationship between Christianity and culture, as the tension between the Reformation and the Renaissance makes very clear; and it has often been the case that a negative attitude to culture has developed, in which the apostolic words, 'Love not the world, neither the things that are in the world' (1 John 2:15) have been taken to mean that the two stand in antithesis to one another. This has led to all sorts of tensions and many most unfortunate attitudes developing in the lives of Christian people, amounting at times to a denial of common humanity. The words of the Roman poet and playwright Terence are very relevant in this regard, and require to be taken with all seriousness:

Homo sum; humani nil a me alienum puto
I am a man, I count nothing human indifferent to me.

If, as Calvin and the Reformers insisted, salvation is a restoring of our lost humanity, and a return to a substantial integrity of life, it is difficult to see how ordinary human, cultural interests and activities can be regarded as wrong or dangerous. We must beware, says Donald MacLeod, in the article already referred to, of stigmatising ordinary recreational and cultural pursuits as if they led directly to hell.

It was impressive to hear a distinguished Christian leader some time ago tell of a survey carried out in the missionary situation in China before the revolution, in which it was discovered that missionaries who had no cultural interests outside their work tended to crack up far more - and far more quickly - than those who did have such interests. This is an immensely important and significant consideration, and it serves to underline the necessity of giving our Christianity a human face. This is a point finely made by C.S. Lewis in a sermon preached at Oxford at the beginning of the Second World War, entitled 'Learning in War-time', in which he argues that it is impossible to suspend or deny one's whole intellectual and aesthetic pursuits as a Christian in the desire to make Christ all in all in one's life, and that to attempt to do so would only succeed in substituting a worse cultural life for a better.

> You are not, in fact, going to read nothing... if you don't read good books you will read bad ones. If you don't go on thinking rationally, you will think irrationally. If you reject aesthetic satisfactions you will fall into sensual satisfactions.

It is worthy of comment, in this regard, that the Apostle Paul, whose total dedication as a Christian is well expressed in the words, 'To me to live is Christ', was evidently not without intellectual and cultural interests.

It is true that the Frenchman Renan desparaged him as a cultural Philistine, saying, 'The ugly little Jew abused Greek art by describing the statues as idols.' Paul was not in Athens as a tourist, but as an ambassador for Christ; and there are some things more important than culture for a man who has the souls of

men on his heart. And yet, in the sermon he preached
to the Athenians on Mars Hill, we find him quoting the
Greek poets 'off the cuff', a practice not ordinarily
associated with cultural Philistines.

The need for balance, whether in matters of
Christian experience, or in doctrine, or in one's
attitude to culture, is clearly an important consideration and one that when neglected or ill-understood can
prove a fruitful source of despondency and spiritual depression; and the answer to the Psalmist's question,
"Why art thou cast down, O my soul?" can on occasion be found in a careful appraisal of what we have
tried to delineate in this chapter.

16

A FRESH GRIP ON LIFE

Hebrews 12:12: "Take a fresh grip on life and brace your trembling limbs" (J.B. Phillips).

We come in this chapter to a consideration of the kind of despondency and discouragement that can develop when we think that life is being rather hard on us, and trial - of whatever sort - is pressing us very severely. There is inevitably some measure of overlap in these studies, as indeed there is in the Scripture passages on which they are based. For example, we could equally well have taken the first chapter of 1 Peter instead of Hebrews chapter twelve as the basis for this chapter, for the thought in the two passages is much the same.

Peter wrote his first epistle in a desire to say something to hard-pressed believers that would encourage them to hold fast, and to stand firm under pressure; and this is what the writer to the Hebrews is also intent upon doing, as he addresses himself to believers who were stumbling and faltering, and likely to fall away from the Faith under the pressures that had come upon them.

What Peter says is,

Now for a season, if need be, ye are in heaviness through manifold temptations: that the trial of your faith, being much more precious than of gold that perisheth, though it be tried with fire, might be found unto praise and honour and glory at the appearing of Jesus Christ. (1 Peter 1:6,7)

We shall look in some detail at this passage, particularly the idea of 'the trial of your faith', in our next chapter, but we take these words as our starting point now in launching out into the twelfth chapter of the epistle to the Hebrews.

Peter interprets the trials and pressures that come upon believers as a trial of faith; and merely to do this is to bring illumination and light to the whole situation, and to put a certain construction upon it, which gives the experience of pressure some meaning. And as long as it has meaning, all is not darkness, and we can go on and bear it. This is exactly the approach that the writer to the Hebrews takes, especially in 12:3-13, a passage which richly repays careful study. The whole chapter indeed is a notable statement, in which the writer unfolds what we may call a number of incentives to steadfastness of life in the midst of many differing pressures. The message surely is, 'He is able to keep you from falling' (Jude 24). These incentives are as follows:

Firstly in vv.1-3: The example and sufficiency of Christ - looking unto Jesus, an outward look to the objective facts of the Divine revelation; an upward look to our Divine destiny, the measure of the stature of the fulness of Christ; a forward look to greater disclosures our Lord has yet to make.

It is important, however, for us to be clear about what 'looking to Jesus' really means. It is not 'Jesus as an example to follow' that is in view. As James Denney rightly says,

The subject of the apostle's gospel was not Jesus the carpenter of Nazareth, but Christ the Lord of glory; men, as he understood the matter, were saved, not by dwelling on the wonderful words and deeds of One who had lived some time ago, and reviving these in their imagination, but by receiving the almighty, emancipating, quickening Spirit of One who lived and reigned for evermore. The transformation here spoken of is not the work of a powerful imagination, which can make the figure in the pages of the Gospels live again, and suffuse the soul with feeling as it gazes upon it; preach this as gospel who will, it was never preached by an apostle of Jesus Christ. It is the work of the Spirit, and the Spirit is given, not to the memory or imagination which can vivify the past, but to the faith which sees Christ upon his throne. *And it is subject to the condition of faith in the living Christ that contemplation of Jesus in the Gospels changes us into the same image.*

It is the faith which sees Christ upon his throne that is in view.

Secondly in vv.4-11: Understanding the meaning of the trial, and the purpose of the 'chastening'.

Thirdly in vv.12-17: A warning about the consequences of failure.

Fourthly in vv.18-24: The privilege of the new covenant.

Fifthly in vv.25ff..: He has spoken to us! 'See that ye refuse not him that speaketh.'

Such is the structure of the chapter, and it will serve to provide a framework for our thinking about what is underlined in vv.3-13, about understanding the meaning and purpose of the trial and the chastening.

The first thing here is to recognise that trial, pressure, testing - call it what we will - is an integral part of Christian experience, and that one cannot be a Christian without encountering this in some shape or form. In this regard, it is worth noticing that in the words "the race that is set before us", the word 'race' in the Greek is the word from which we get our word 'agony' (elsewhere translated as 'contest'), and that the phrase 'set before us' translates a Greek word which could be fairly rendered 'it is already there'. The pressure, the contest, the agony, is present at the outset of our commitment to Christ, and as soon as ever we engage to be the Lord's and begin the Christian life pressure, of one kind or another, is straightaway a reality for us.

It is by no means unnecessary to underline this today, for there are those who would maintain that battling is a sign that we are not getting through to fulness of Christian living. We simply point out that this is not a scriptural viewpoint. The apostle Peter says (1 Pet 4:12), "Think it not strange concerning the fiery trial which is to try you, as though some strange thing happened unto you...." It is not a strange thing for a Christian to encounter trial, nor is it a sign that there is something wrong with his faith either; rather it is something integral to Christian experience. "In the world," said Jesus, "ye have tribulation" (John 16:33).

The second thing for us to note is something that is

made very explicit in other parts of Scripture as, for example, in the first two chapters of the book of Job, namely, the interaction of the work of Satan and the permission and ordination of God in trial. The pressures that come upon Christians may certainly issue from Satan, and have their origin in his evil designs against us (cf Matt 13:28, "An enemy hath done this"), but God nevertheless permits them, and indeed ordains them, and uses them for his own ends. We could put it like this: Satan may fire the arrow, but God sovereignly intercepts it in mid-flight, as it were, and extracts the poison from its tip, so that by the time it reaches us its warhead has been disarmed, and it becomes fraught with blessing for us.

But - although that may be so - a certain attitude to it now becomes all-important. We must realise that God is in it - hence the writer's excursus on the meaning of chastening. The thing does not work automatically; and it is possible to have a wrong attitude to it (we will deal with that in some detail presently) and allow it to embitter us - the Apostle recognises this possibility later in the passage (v15). This, it will be remembered, is how it was with Naomi, Ruth's mother-in-law, who allowed chastening to turn her into a bitter old woman. How sad that this should happen! But we know that it often does, to the hurt not only of those who fall victim to it, but also of those around them.

In the next place we are to realise that the word 'chastening' translates a Greek word 'paidaia', which literally means 'education' ('discipline' is how the RSV and the NIV render it). There is a rather wonderful thought in this: God turns Satan's attacks upon his children into education for them. We could well call the theme of this chapter 'with Christ in the school of suffering'. Chastening, when we have the right attitude to it, is educative. And if we pursue the metaphor a little, we could go on to say this: sometimes children are difficult and fractious in school, and will not learn their lessons, so that their teacher is obliged to 'keep them in' after school hours, to go over the lesson once again with them. Indeed, in extreme cases, pupils have been known to have been 'kept back' to repeat a year, when the other children go forward. This prompts the reflection that we sometimes suffer longer as Christians than we need to, because of our slowness to learn the lessons God is concerned to teach us: we are 'kept in', or 'kept back' to repeat the process!

The Apostle seeks to underline this truth by referring his readers to the Scriptures, drawing their attention to what is said in the third chapter of the Book of Proverbs, which we shall do well to consider. Significantly, the context of this passage in Proverbs is the theme of wisdom. The writer has already, in chapter 2, stressed the moral stability of life that grows with wisdom, and in the next chapter emphasises the serenity and peace that come through wisdom. The association of the process of chastening in 3:11 with what follows in 13-18 about the fruit of that chastening in the attainment of wisdom - "Her ways are the ways of pleasantness, and all her paths are peace" - is exactly paralleled in the Apostle's words in 12:11,

Now no chastening for the present seemeth to be joyous, but grievous: nevertheless afterward it yieldeth the peaceable fruit of righteousness unto them which are exercised thereby.

The peaceable fruit of righteousness - this is the result of the chastening, the educative process. God is intent upon producing character and integrity in us, and chastening is one of the ways in which he does this. We are all involved in the battle for character, and this is the real answer to be given to the anguished question we sometimes ask, "Oh God, why are you doing this to me?" God is using the discipline of chastening to put mettle into us. And so he directs us to Scripture and invites us to allow Scripture to interpret these experiences to us.

This passage in Proverbs teaches us that there are two 'wrong reactions' to pressures. In the first place, we are not to despise the chastening of the Lord, in the sense of remaining blind to its meaning and purpose, and failing to see the hand of God in it. Rather we must be like Job and pray, "That which I see not teach thou me" (Job 34:32). In the second place, we are warned not to faint under the chastening, and crumple and go to pieces. Rather, by faith we are to see that in the midst of it God is on the throne, and rightly to relate oneself to it. This is important, for if we do not rightly relate to it, black discouragement is likely to set in, and this is almost a greater problem in the Christian life than sin - in this sense: if a man falls into sin, he can weep his way back to the cross and find forgiveness and restoration: but if he falls into despondency and discouragement, his attitude may become "What is the use of going on? I might as well give up;" and he does not come to Christ for help, but wallows in his darkness. That is a very serious state to be in, and explains the Apostle's concern in exhorting us to listen to what God says to us on this subject.

Next, the Apostle goes on to say that trials and pressures are no cause for despondency; rather, they attest our relationship as sons and daughters of the Father. He deals with us as his children, and it is fatherly discipline that is being exercised. The disquieting thing in this regard would be if we did not experience chastening, for this would be to call in question our status as children of the Father.

The next step in the writer's argument is a comparison and contrast between the attitude of natural parents and that of God the Father. The point he is making seems to be that if natural children are prepared to submit to family discipline, even if they may feel it is harsh or unjust, God's children should much more be prepared to submit to their Father's correction, since they must know that he always deals with them justly and in love. Human parents may be misguided in their treatment of their children, though well-meaning - the words in the Authorised Version rendering 'after their own pleasure' are better translated 'as it seemed good to them' - and no human parent is perfect; all alike make mistakes. But this is never so with God: he can be relied on never to impose what is not good for us. The words of the hymn are always true:

My Father's hand will never cause
His child a needless tear.

His thoughts towards us are thoughts of peace, and not of evil (Jer. 29:11). It is always safe to assume that God's discipline of us is never inappropriate, never out of place, but always for our profit - even when it may have been brought upon us by some human inconsideration, or callousness, or some attitude of wilfulness, or by some evil mind. God means it for our profit, and he presses it into service that we may become partakers of his holiness. It is true that the experience of this may be deeply painful and grievous, leading even to heartbreak; but there is an 'afterward', as both the Apostle and the writer of Proverbs make abundantly clear: "Happy is the man" who tastes "the peaceable fruit of righteousness" which results from a true attitude and response to the discipline of grace.

Because this is so, the Apostle issues the resounding exhortation, "Lift up the hands which hang down, and the feeble knees," which J.B. Phillips graphically paraphrases, "Take a fresh grip on life and brace your trembling limbs." It is significant that the Apostle is once again directing his readers to the Scriptures, for his words are taken from Isaiah 35:3ff., a passage which also underlines the reality of the 'afterward'. Hearts in the grip of bleak discouragement need no word so much as this; and to see the purpose and intention of God in the trials we endure will go a long way towards bracing our spirits. The word 'straight' in the phrase, 'make straight paths for your feet,' has the force of 'going in the right direction.' One might think of a ploughman ploughing a straight furrow by keeping his eyes fixed on the post at the far side of the field. Some have thought that there may be a suggestion of the very winding path that Israel took on the way to the Promised Land, at the end of which they were turned back into the wilderness at Kadesh because of their unbelief. They did not learn the lessons of their chastening and discipline, but murmured against God and were finally "turned out of the way" (v.13). The modern translations of this verse - particularly J.B. Phillips', which reads, "on the right path the limping foot recovers strength" - seem to suggest that there is a healing power at work on the right way.

In the context of our present study, 'the right way' must be understood as the way unfolded in the Scriptures the Apostle has referred to - that of not despising the chastening of the Lord, not fainting under his rebuke, but rather discerning and recognising the purpose in his dealings with us as being full of grace, and holding an 'afterward' that is bright with promise for the deepening and enrichment of our lives and their enduement for further and fruitful service.

17

THE TRIAL OF FAITH

1 Peter 1:6,7: "Now for a season, if need be, ye are in heaviness through manifold temptations: that the trial of your faith... might be found unto praise and honour and glory..."

We have made reference more than once in previous chapters to the apostle Peter's words about the trial of faith. There is a sense in which that phrase could well have been taken as the motto text of the whole book, and it will be useful to look at it now in some detail to see something of what is implied and involved in it.

By way of introduction, we should note the setting that Peter gives to the theme of the trial of faith: it is hedged in on both sides by an emphasis on the reality of the Christian hope. The passage in which the words occur begins with a doxology which magnifies the mercy by which we are begotten "unto a lively hope," and it is followed by the exhortation, "Gird up the loins of the mind, be sober, and hope to the end, for the grace that is to be brought unto you at the revelation of Jesus Christ."

That is to say, all our experience of trial and testing

as Christians has to be understood in the context of the Christian hope which, as the writer to the Hebrews says (6:19) is "an anchor of the soul, both sure and steadfast." This, for the Christian, is always the deepest truth, and a constant factor in his experience. And one of the marvellous things about this hope is that, future though it may be in its essence, the grace that is in it for the believer percolates backwards into time, and over-shadows us in all the way that we take. In the trial of our faith, we are meant to understand, grace comes to us from the hope that is ours in Christ, and this means that we can never ultimately despair. The hope is always there.

As was pointed out briefly in the last chapter, Peter speaks of the trials and pressures that come upon believers, and interprets them, as a trial of faith. And merely to do this is to bring illumination and light to the whole situation, and put a new complexion upon it altogether. It gives the experience meaning, and so long as it has meaning, all is not darkness and we can go on and bear it, especially since it serves to prepare us and equip us for the inheritance that lies before us. And if it does this, we may well rejoice in it.

We sometimes hear it said, of pressures and testings, that 'these things are sent to try us'. And it is so. But we must be careful what we mean here. Faith is being tried, yes; but from whose point of view, and by whom? Who does the trying? It is God. He has the initiative in all this. We should note Peter's words "if need be" in this connection. He does not mean merely that the trial is a possibility, in the sense that circumstances may make it inevitable. Rather, it is the use of the word 'need' which has the force of a Divine necessity (in the same way in which we are told in John 4:4 that Jesus "must needs" go through Samaria). It is all part of the Divine plan. It is necessary.

On the other hand the temptation or trial is set in the context of the Divine foreknowledge and election. It is not merely that he allows or permits the trial, but that he ordains it. This, paradoxically, is a source of comfort and encouragement to believers more than anything else, since it means that the trial and all its course is in God's hands. This is the setting Peter gives to the whole concept of trial.

We may also take into consideration other kindred statements on the subject of testing and trial, such as the following:

Gen. 22:1 - "And it came to pass that God did tempt Abraham..."

Luke 22:31 - "Simon, Simon, Satan hath desired to have thee..."

James 1:2 - "Count it all joy when ye enter into divers temptations..."

James 1:13 - "Let no man say when he is tempted, I am tempted of God; for God cannot be tempted of evil, neither tempteth he any man..."

These are simply a random selection of statements and many other such could be quoted. But two things in particular will be seen in such references: first of all, that temptation is used generally in the wider and, etymologically, more accurate sense of trial or testing rather than of incitement to sin; and in the second place, that there is a complex and subtle interaction between God and the devil in the whole matter. This is seen supremely in the story of Job, and is the point made in the Prologue to that wonderful book. It is Satan who tempts

Job, and yet God not only permits it, but ordains it, and makes use of it for his own sovereign purposes.

There are other instances of this in Scripture which make it clear that Job's experience is no isolated incident. We may take, for example, the story of Joseph in the book of Genesis, this precocious and insufferable young man who roused the ire of all his brothers and stirred them so violently in their passions against him that they sold him into Egypt - an incident which marked the beginning of a period of many years of hard and exacting trials and tribulations for him. Yet at the end of the story he is able to say to his brothers, who had been the instrumental cause of so much of it, "God meant it unto good." Thirteen years of captivity in Egypt, with some of these spent in prison - and "God meant it unto good!"

Another example is seen in the apostle Paul's hazardous experience in Jerusalem, and afterwards in prison in Rome, towards the end of his missionary career. In the light of all that he passed through - the riots in Jerusalem, when he was nearly torn limb from limb by the enraged and infuriated Jews; the plot against his life that was discovered only just in time; the tremendous storm experience in the Aegean Sea; and his captivity in Rome - he could yet write a letter from that prison and say to the Philippians, "I would that ye should understand, brethren, that the things which happened unto me have fallen out rather unto the furtherance of the gospel" (Phil. 1:12).

Clearly, then, God's sovereign hand is always in control. He calls the tune. This seems to be implied in the Paul's words, "God is faithful, who will not suffer you to be tempted above that ye are able..." (1 Cor. 10:13).

There is something of great importance for us to learn in this, namely, that we are not always the best judge of the situation, or of just how much we are able to endure in any particular trial - as may be graphically illustrated from these scriptural instances themselves.

We can hardly suppose that there were not times, during Joseph's thirteen year continuing trial in Egypt and in the prison there, when he felt he had had enough, and was being asked to bear more than was humanly possible. He was, to use Paul's words in 2 Corinthians 1:8, "pressed out of measure, above strength," and he may well have said, perhaps many times, "I cannot stand any more." But God said, quietly, "Yes, you can, my son," and dared to leave him in the trial.

And must there not have been times when Job felt all he wanted to do was to die and escape from his misery? Yet God left him there for so long. And what of Paul's experience in Corinth, in Acts 18, when he must have felt he could not stay a day longer in that evil and debauched city - yet God reassured him by a vision, saying, "Be not afraid, but speak, and hold not thy peace; for I am with thee, and no man shall set thee to hurt thee...," and he remained there for a further eighteen months.

Some very pertinent things can be said about all this. First of all, the fact of trial and testing is an integral part of the believer's life. This is everywhere evident, in the Scriptures and in spiritual experience alike. "In the world," said Jesus to his disciples, "ye have tribulation," and he was bearing witness in so saying to an unalterable law in spiritual life. Basically, this is because his kingdom is not of this world, and those who are his are travelling in a diametrically opposite direction to that of the world. Of course there will be clashes. It is the collision of two worlds that a believer is involved in, and sooner or later - and at all sorts of points in his experience - that collision is something he will know to his cost. One has only to look at the history of the Early Church, and the opposition and persecution that was stirred up against the first Christians, to see the truth of this. At times it seemed as though all hell was let loose against them. Yet they rejoiced in it, and counted it all joy. "We glory in tribulations," says Paul in Romans 5:3. How could they do something that was so much against natural considerations? This brings us to our second point.

The tribulation comes from the powers that are arrayed against the gospel, but God has a purpose in it, and uses it, making capital out of it. And that purpose is that the trial of our faith, "being much more precious than of gold that perisheth... might be found unto praise and honour and glory at the appearing of Jesus Christ" - in this regard that trial, in the providence of God, does something to people. "Tribulation," says Paul, "worketh character." This is exactly God's purpose, and why he not only allows it but ordains it - and when we look at it in this sense we have to say that he ordains it. It is not a question of God accidentally taking up something that is in existence already and deciding that since it is already there he might as well make use of it. On the contrary, he calls the tune and it is important that we should see this to be so.

One sees this emphasis throughout the New Testament, and particularly in Paul's writings, as for example in the famous passage in Ephesians 4:8ff., where he speaks of our being brought to maturity in Christ, and of the measure of the stature of his fulness, of our being made perfect, not in the sense of being made sinless but of being brought into our true and proper destiny in the mind and intention of God, through the disciplines of the Word.

Peter himself speaks at the end of his first epistle of being prepared for glory through suffering (5:10) and, as we have already seen, the writer to the Hebrews spends a whole chapter dealing with this theme, pointing out that chastening is something so integral to the experience of the children of God that it may be doubted whether they are his at all if they do not pass through it. God has his eye on the finished product, that men might be to the praise and honour and glory of his great Name, and this is accomplished only through the disciplines of grace.

The trial is putting faith to the test to see of what sort it is, and to put steel and temper into it, so as to make it a massive and substantial reality that will bring glory and praise to God - this is the point of the exercise. We are often too easily satisfied with what we think God may be making of us. But he is not. He is intent that the work shall be thorough, and he spares no effort to make it so.

C.S. Lewis makes a very perceptive comment in this connection:

God has not been trying an experiment on my faith or love in order to find out their quality. He knew it already. It was I who didn't. In this trial, he makes us occupy the dock, the witness box and the bench all at once. He always knew that my temple was a house

189

of cards. His only way of making me realise the fact was to knock it down.

The thought of being put to the test to let us see what we are made of is a very telling one, for it means that part of the function of trial is to expose all that is unreal in us, to strip away every false foundation and false superstructure in our lives, in order that true foundations and true superstructures may be built.

This is surely evident in the story of Joseph's experience. That brash young man's temple was certainly a house of cards, and it had to be knocked down, bringing Joseph down with it. But the wonderful thing is - and we can see this is a way that Joseph could not possibly have seen then - that in all the fierce and fiery trial that came upon him God was intent on building something real and substantial in him that was in the end to be indestructible. The dreams he dreamed as a young man all came true, but at a price, and the trial of his faith was involved in making them come true.

The fact is that faith, even when it is real and genuine, as it is in the true believer, often tends to gather parasitic accretions, which are a hindrance to its growth and development. These must be cut away ruthlessly, if we are to be adequately prepared to enter our inheritance. As Jesus puts it in John 15:2, "Every branch that beareth fruit, he purgeth it that it may bring forth more fruit." Anything false that may inadvertently attach itself to our faith is a potential danger to our spiritual lives. Hence the fire - only the pure gold can stand it; it is purified, and the rest is destroyed.

But we cannot always see the meaning and purpose of our testing, even in retrospect. One of the most remarkable things about Job's experience is that in the answer God gave to his cries and tears no explanation was given of the mystery of his sufferings, and no answers to any of his questions. But God answered him, which is infinitely more important. The truth of the matter is that there are some trials that are not explained to us, not ever in this life. The answer lies with God, and we may not demand that he explain himself to us. This may be very hard; but it is something we must accept. He giveth not account of any of his matters.

This leads us to a consideration of what could be called the resoluteness of God. There is a sense in which it could be said that there is a grimness about the Divine love. God does not spare his children. He is strong enough to resist pity when we cry out in pain, until pain has done its gracious work in us. We see an example of this in Paul's words in 2 Corinthians 1:8ff., already referred to, about being "pressed out of measure, above strength, insomuch that we despaired even of life," and having "the sentence of death in ourselves." But the result was an utter trust in God. If Paul was human at all, he must have cried out in pain at that experience, and there must have been moments when his plaint was, "O God, this is too much, why are you allowing this to happen to me?" But the extremity of the testing and trial served to produce a quality of trust in him that nothing else could. This is what we mean by the resoluteness of God's dealings with his people! He knows what he is after, and will not let up, because his eyes are on the end-product. What he wanted in this situation was an utterly believing man, and he could accomplish this only in one way, by pressing Paul out of measure and above strength.

We can speak of something else also, in addition to the resoluteness of God's dealings with his people: the daring of God. How utterly daring he is in the things he does with us and to us! He is not afraid to thrust us into the fire, and to leave us there until we feel we have passed the point of endurance. Sometimes the thought that comes to our hearts, and perhaps even on our lips, in such a situation is, "How dare you do this to me!" And the answer is, he is a daring God, and that is why he dares to do it. And he is daring, because he is so big: there is nothing little about him. And if he is such a God, big and daring, and incredibly alive with Divine energy and virtue, creative and transforming, it is hardly surprising that sparks should fly when that energy comes into contact with our lives. It is not possible but that we should feel it in some way, or that it should leave its mark upon us.

The story of Jacob wrestling with the angel (Gen. 32:24ff.) is a case in point. The patriarch was never the same again after such an experience. The angel touched his thigh, and the sinew of his thigh shrank, and he was crippled for life. Do we really think that wrestling with God would be fun? It was a terrible experience for Jacob, but it made him a prince with God. And his faith was "found unto praise and honour and glory."

Why such daring on God's part? Is he not afraid that his people might crumble? Two things may be said in answer to this. The first is that in such an experience it is always true that he says, "When thou passest through the waters, I will be with thee; and through the rivers, they shall not overflow thee: when thou walkest through the fire, thou shalt not be burned; neither shall the flame kindle upon thee. Fear not!" (Is. 43:1,2). The second thing to be said is that God is daring because he is so sovereign. He plays with the opposition. And it plays into his hands; he is so completely in control that he is always several moves ahead, like a master chess player who simply smiles when his opponent thinks he has trapped him; for whatever move he makes, the master is going to win in the end.

One thinks, for example, of the easy sovereignty that God displayed in the story of the deliverance of his people from Egypt in the time of the Exodus. His people were crying for help, and the heavens seemed to be as brass, with no answer coming. But all the time, God had sent a little baby to a Levite family, and that was his answer to the plight of his people in Egypt, because this baby was in the fulness of time to be the deliverer. Pharaoh decreed that all the Israelites' male children should be slain, in a characteristic act of barbarity and cruelty, but the story reveals how easily God snapped his fingers in that situation.

This is what we mean by the daring of God: not only did he arrange for the preservation of Moses in the basket in the bulrushes, but he actually decreed that his anointed and appointed deliverer should be brought up in the court of that murderous king. Was that not a daring, even audacious thing for God to do? We almost find ourselves, in reading of it, crying out, "O God, you cannot do that, it is too dangerous!" But things that are too dangerous for us God does almost casually. That is how completely in control he is.

When we begin to think in these terms, we begin to see something of the greatness and the majesty of this God with whom we have to do, and we begin to see something else that we had not seen before, about our own trials. For if that is the kind of God who is dealing with us, we need not be afraid, still less do we need to complain.

The idea of discipline doing something to our lives is well illustrated by the story of the Syro-Phoenecian woman, in Matthew 15:21-29. Here, if anywhere, is a record of the trial and triumph of faith. This woman came (we are told in Mark that she came because she had heard of Jesus; word had got around about him, and faith comes by hearing) because she felt instinctively that here was someone who could help her in her extremity of need. She ran to him, pleading and crying, "Have mercy on me, O Lord, thou son of David; my daughter is grievously vexed with a devil." And he ignored her! He cut her dead. It is one of the most astonishing things recorded in Scripture. Then, when she persisted in her pleading, he rebuffed her, saying, "I am not sent but unto the lost sheep of the house of Israel." She did not belong to the chosen people. But again she persisted, "Lord, help me," to which he replied, "It is not meet to take the children's bread, and to cast it to dogs." That was a hard one, was it not, from the lips of the Son of God? A woman, weeping her heart out about her daughter at the point of death - and the Son of God spoke like this, virtually calling her a dog! But even this did not repel her, and still she came back, and - we may say it reverently - she was a match for him. "Truth, Lord," she said, "yet the dogs eat of the crumbs from their master's table."

And this is what the Son of God wanted to hear. The reason why he cut her dead at the beginning was not because he was not interested, but because he was testing her. The reason why he rebuffed her was not to dismiss her heartlessly, but to see how real her faith was. And when he spoke of the impropriety of casting the children's bread to dogs, it was the supreme and final test. It was the strength of the Divine compassion withholding itself until faith blossomed into fruition. When she came back to him with her magnificent, final reposte, the smile broke on his face, and what an experience it must have been for the woman to see that marvellous smile, and to know that faith had triumphed through the trial and because of it. "O woman, great is thy faith," he said to her, "be it unto thee even as thou wilt."

There is often a real battle before faith is enabled to gain hold of God. This is the point of the discipline, and this is why God sometimes seems to play 'hard to get' - not because he is tormenting people, but because he loves them, and is intent on drawing them out to see of what stuff they are made. So it was with the woman: faith, real faith, was called forth, formed and established, by the very trial that Jesus imposed upon her.

She was in a desperate state, it is true; but this is the whole point of the exercise, for what God does to us in testing and trial is best described by the apostle Paul when he speaks of being "shut up unto faith" (Gal. 3:23). This is always true: in every case, trial makes for the utter casting of oneself upon God as the only alternative to despair. This is God's purpose in it, and why he tests his people.

Martin Luther once said, "God made the world out of nothing, and it is only when we are nothing that he can make something of us." It is when we are brought to an end of ourselves by testing that God can do something with us. It is always when we are at the end of the road, no longer trusting in ourselves, that God can raise us from the dead. Saul of Tarsus is brought to an end of himself down in the dust of the Damascus Road before God can raise him to newness of life; the Prodigal Son sinks to destitution in the far country, deserted by his friends and feeding on the husks of the swine before he is able to say, "I will arise and go to my father."

All that has been said must surely serve to set the 'heaviness' of which Peter speaks in its true and proper context, bringing illumination upon the dark passages of life that are the common experience of God's people, enabling us to see that the trial of our faith has been allowed and ordained by him in order to meet us in grace. This is what makes the trial "much more precious than of gold that perisheth, though it be tried with fire." And what Peter goes on to say is of profound significance: "Whom having not seen, ye love; in whom, though now ye see him not, yet believing, ye rejoice with joy unspeakable and full of glory" (1 Peter 1:8). The message of these words is this: the testing and trial are designed to bring us closer to Christ. We are pressed into fellowship and communion with the Son of God; and this, Peter means to indicate, is a means of strengthening and stabilising in times of pressure. And if the trial of our faith leads to this, it is of rare value indeed.

18

THE ACCUSER OF THE BRETHREN

Matthew 13:28: "An enemy hath done this."

No study on the subject of spiritual depression could be regarded as exhaustive or complete without some mention being made of one further issue, namely, the activity of the evil one in this whole realm, and his significance as a factor in both the understanding of, and in the effectual dealing with, depression. We look at this now in our concluding chapter - not indeed as an afterthought, or because it is of lesser importance than what has already been considered, for it has in fact relevance to everything that has been said so far, and provides a dark backcloth against which to see the subject all the more clearly.

It is quite certain that from a pastoral point of view no adequate counselling can be given without taking into consideration the reality of satanic influence in human experience. It can hardly be doubted that there are states and conditions of spiritual depression about which the truest thing that could be said of them is that "an enemy hath done this." Nor should this surprise us, for the writers of the New Testament make it very clear that behind the seen world there is an unseen world of spirits, dark and evil powers with strong and malignant personality, planning the destruction of the souls of men; and for these writers this was no mere form of words, but a grim and terrible reality.

Since this is so, it should surely be taken as basic that the element of the demonic must be regarded as a relevant and inevitable factor in a true understanding of this important area of experience. It is a measure of how much the idea of the demonic has become - to use Professor James S. Stewart's words in a responsible theological journal - "a neglected emphasis in New Testament theology" - that its influence should be so substantially discounted as a serious consideration in much of our contemporary theological and pastoral thinking about depression. This neglect has been widespread and far-reaching, with what disastrous results we may not as yet be fully aware.

It is perhaps a more hopeful sign in the theological scene that one of the foremost theologians of the twentieth century, Dr. Emil Brunner, writes in a notable chapter entitled 'Angels, Spirits and the Devil':

What the Bible says plainly is this: that there is a power of darkness, and that it is of great significance. As a force of a superhuman kind it stands over against men. It is an 'objective reality', that is, it is a reality which is objectively encountered, not merely a reality within the mind. It is a purely spiritual force, which works directly upon the spirit... Its method of influence is 'occult'..." (Dogmatics, II, pp.133ff..)

And Brunner adds,

> It is precisely those great Christians who have the deepest experience who have the greatest personal experience of the reality of the power of darkness.

Nevertheless, Brunner, along with others, warns against allowing all this to run riot, and says,

> Any such doctrine, unless kept within the strictest bounds, could produce disastrous results comparable to the whole sorry story of witch-hunting in the Middle Ages.

This is a very salutary warning. There are, in fact, two opposite dangers in this whole field. One is an undue preoccupation with the fact of Satan, which tends to overshadow and even eclipse the real biblical emphasis, namely, that the most important truth about the devil is this: Jesus Christ has conquered him. This is the uniform and consistent testimony of the Scriptures, and it is not in order for Christian people to be so preoccupied with Satan and his demons that they lose sight of this healthy and wholesome biblical testimony. To do so not only serves to discredit the real biblical doctrine, but can also prove ultimately disintegrative of spiritual life itself, as well as undermining the reality of human responsibility. For nowhere in Scripture is it ever suggested the power of the devil is irresistible or that it is of such a kind as to negate human responsibility. The devil leads men astray, he suggests evil; but the man who allows himself to be led astray and to be incited to evil is wholly responsible for his own actions.

That is the one extreme; and the other is simply to deride the whole concept of a personal power of evil and to deny the existence of the reality of the demonic altogether. We may say that those who take such a view are being jolted out of it by what is happening in society today, and into a puzzled and perplexed awareness of a dimension in human experience which they have hitherto discounted. It is hardly surprising that a generation that has experienced such diabolical wickedness as ours has - even as this is being written reports have appeared in the press of a Member of Parliament compiling a dossier of evidence of human sacrifice being made in different parts of Britain by witches' covens - should be abandoning their former 'enlightened' objection to the existence of a 'power of darkness', and are now prepared to believe in Satan as represented in the Bible.

The New Testament is clear and unequivocal in its emphasis here. It speaks unmistakeably about the reality of the dark powers, and of Christ's victory and triumph over them in his Cross and Resurrection. But that conquest of the evil one does not put him out of existence; rather, he has been deprived of his power, in the same way as the two lions at the gate of the Palace Beautiful in Bunyan's *Pilgrim's Progress* were rendered harmless by being chained, so that although Christian heard them roar as he went forward, they did him no harm. If, however, he had ventured within the radius of their chains, it would have been a very different matter.

Not only, however, does the New Testament speak of the reality of the dark powers against which we wrestle (Eph. 6:10ff.), but it also is very specific about the kind of influence they can exercise in the lives of men. "We are not ignorant of his devices," says Paul in 2 Corinthians 2:11; but many, alas, are; and such ignorance can cost a great deal in this particular realm of spiritual depression. This is why it is important for us to study the more detailed teaching of the New Testament about the evil one and his wiles.

The first thing to recognise is the sphere in which the spiritual warfare, of which Paul speaks, is waged. It is "in the heavenly places" (Eph. 6:12). This has something significant to tell us. At the beginning of the Ephesian epistle Paul speaks of the believer's position in Christ as being "blessed with all spiritual blessings in heavenly places in Christ" (1:3). When that position is realised in experience, and becomes the believer's possession, through a true consecration, it is precisely then that warfare with the powers of darkness is encountered. Sometimes, it is true, the enemy plays havoc with us when we are careless and slack spiritually; but in this sense it is more often the case that he attacks when we are truly and deeply consecrated. The old Puritan was right when he said, "He that stands near to his captain is a sure target for the archers," and this is underlined in different words by Samuel Chadwick, the Methodist saint, "Every man's Pentecost is a signal for Satan to gird himself."

If, then, it is at the place of consecration that the battleground is set, the situation becomes fraught with peril when there is ignorance of Satan's wiles.

In this connection, it is helpful, as well as necessary, to recognise that while Satan is behind all sin, the Scriptures indicate that temptation to sin is not the only wile that the evil one uses to harm souls. And it is as well that we should recognize his other forms of activity also.

One of the names given to Satan in the New Testament is Apollyon (Rev. 9:11), which means 'the Destroyer'. This bears witness to the disintegrative and destructive nature of the evil one's working in the lives of men. In a day when we hear reports of Satanist groups and 'churches' who deliberately and of set purpose pray to the devil that he would ruin the living work of God in a community, with the result that there has been breakdown in the health of God's servants, and breakdown of marriages, leading to invalidism and resignation, this description of 'the Destroyer' seems particularly apt. He is a ruthless enemy whose will is to destroy without mercy.

This also serves to explain some of the dark and terrifying experiences through which believers sometimes pass, experiences in which they feel as if they are being 'torn apart'. One thinks of Christian in Bunyan's *Pilgrim's Progress,* as he passed through the Valley of the Shadow, and was enveloped in a horror of great darkness and endured such spiritual turmoil, oppression and confusion that his mind seemed like to be destroyed. The story of the man with the legion of devils in Mark 5, with its graphic picture of the disintegration of human personality, may have much to teach us here.

Another aspect of Satan's working is seen in 1 Thessalonians 2:18, where the apostle Paul refers to him as a 'hinderer'. "Satan," he says, "hindered me." This is not simply a form of words, equivalent to the phrase we sometimes use, 'Circumstances prevented me.' If the words mean anything, they must surely mean that a definite and specific work was engineered by the evil one, by which the Apostle was, at least temporarily, frustrated in the fulfilment of the will of God. It is not difficult in this context to see how fruitful a cause of depression this could prove to be in the experience of the believer, and how needful it is to be able to recognise its source and deal with it effectively.

We have to be careful here, however, for there were other experiences that Paul passed through, in which he was also hindered, as for example, at the beginning of his second missionary journey (Acts 16:6 ff), where we are told that it was the Spirit of God that forbade him to preach the Word in Asia, and 'suffered him not' to go into Bithynia. The question that arises is how to distinguish between the Spirit of God's constraints and the evil one's hindering.

The apostle John exhorts us, "Believe not every spirit, but try the spirits whether they are of God" (1 John 4:1). This serves to underline and emphasise the saying, 'Know your enemy'. It is very important in spiritual life to be able to discern whether any particular constraint or hindering is from God, in which case we must pay heed to it and submit to it, or from the devil, in which case we must therefore dispute it in the name of our victorious Redeemer.

Evidence of Satan's hindering is not wanting in other areas of spiritual experience. In the realm of unanswered prayer, for example, this could teach us a great deal, as we may gather from the remarkable account, in Daniel 10, of the prophet's perplexing experience in making intercession for his people, when it was revealed to him by the angel of God that from the first day of his fasting and prayer he had been heard, but that an unseen hindrance had been at work - 'the prince of the kingdom of Persia', surely an evil tutelary spirit! - delaying the answer to his prayer. How easy it would have been for the prophet - and how easy for us - to be discouraged and cast down into despondency of spirit, without that knowledge and realisation. And if, as Paul makes clear in 2 Corinthians 4:4, Satanic influence is at work in the minds of unbelievers hindering them from faith in Christ, why should it be supposed unlikely that the same influence can be at work, in the dark depression of spirit that sometimes assails the children of God?

Then again, Satan is represented as 'the accuser of the brethren' (Rev. 12:10). We have already spoken in an earlier chapter of the dark doubts that sometimes assail the believer's spirit, and of the sense of having committed the unpardonable sin. In this deeply distressing experience it is quite certain that, in addition to what was said then, the evil one can give such doubts a subtle twist, intensifying them a hundredfold, and fulfilling the promise of his name as 'accuser', dazing and prostrating the soul with the vehemence of the accusing voices, as they rake up the past, and drive the believer into himself with terrible relentlessness - and never so much as when in prayer and worship - in such a way that, no matter how much or often he 'confesses' his sin, he cannot seem to find rest or peace. He is always 'in the wrong'. And the darkness gets deeper and deeper under such 'conviction' from the evil one until despair settles in the soul.

How needful, therefore, to recognise our enemy in such an experience, and to be courageous enough to dispute and indeed refuse such pressures, recognising them to have been superimposed upon us by an alien spirit intent on doing us grievous harm, and resisting him in the name of the Lord Jesus.

Another fruitful source of discouragement and depression lies in the evil one's activity as 'an angel of light' (2 Cor. 11:14), by which he counterfeits the Spirit of God, bringing impressions, impulses and intimations to the believer's mind that purport to be from God, and causing him to believe that the Lord is leading and guiding him in a particular way. It is a great and important lesson to learn in spiritual life that all spiritual intimations do not necessarily come from the good Spirit of God. It is one of the surest ways to spiritual shipwreck to open the mind indiscriminately to spiritual impulses; and when we fail to heed the apostolic injunction to "try the spirits whether they be of God," nothing is surer than that we shall be plunged into a black discouragement and depression of spirit from which only spiritual light and illumination about the evil one's working can deliver us.

The subtlety of the evil one's masquerading as an angel of light is, of course, that we can so easily be taken in by it. It is not without significance that the word 'serpent' in the Garden of Eden story has been translated by one commentator as 'the shining one'. What if Eve was 'taken in' by the Tempter in his guise as a 'shining one', an angel of light, and that she assumed that it was the voice of God that she heard? The apostle Paul does in fact say that she was 'deceived' (1 Tim. 2:14). What was proposed to her by the evil one was held up as something good, and she was taken in by it.

Merely to recognise the evil one's wiles and devices in this way is already half the battle. It is something, after all, to realise that when we are under such attack, we are not ourselves, and that the strange, frightening experience does not represent the real 'us', but something irrational, and 'from the outside'.

Above all, however - and this is the decisive and all-important consideration - there must be the recognition and the appropriation of the fact that Christ in his death and resurrection has once for all won the victory over all dark powers. He has 'spoiled principalities and powers, making a show of them openly, triumphing over them in' his cross (Col. 2:15). Through death he has "destroyed (in the sense of robbing him of his power) him that had the power of death, that is, the devil" (Heb. 2:14). Calvary was a victory, and in that victory God has put all things under Christ's feet, and made him head over all things to the Church - that is to say, he has made over that victory to us, his people. Indeed, the victory Christ won over the powers of darkness was won for us, and it is given to us to use. This means that we can dispute every evil influence that Satan seeks to exercise over us, and in the name of our victorious Lord bid him be gone from our lives. This is the real heart of the well-known words in Revelation 12:11, "They overcame him (the evil one) by the blood of the Lamb, and by the word of their testimony."

These are the facts of the situation, and faith must lay hold upon them, and put them to the test. Faith must reckon on the reality of Christ's victory over all dark powers, and in that reckoning resist the devil; and he will flee from us (James 4:7). Like a policeman on point duty at the centre of the city, who stops the traffic by the raising of his hand (bearing the authority and majesty of the law), we may also (through Christ's authority given to us to use) stop the flow of unholy traffic through our minds and hearts - whether evil and unhallowed thoughts, doubts and questionings, fears and dreads of different kinds, or any other malevolent wile of Satan. We may dispute its right to torment us, and refuse to be tyrannised by a defeated foe. There is a place in Christian experience for standing firm and saying, "Satan, I dispute your right to torment me, or hinder me, or deceive me. I dispute every evil influence you can exercise over me and I do so in the victorious and triumphant name of my Saviour." This is surely what the apostle Peter meant when he said, "Whom resist, steadfast in the faith" (1 Peter 5:9).

We must therefore read this reality back into every aspect of spiritual depression that we have looked at in these chapters - John the Baptist, Timothy, Elijah, Jonah and all the others - and see the devil's hidden presence, working evil for God's people, and recognise that as another and deeper dimension in which it becomes possible to use the words of the Psalmist, "Hope in God, for I shall yet praise him, who is the health of my countenance, and my God" (Ps.43:5). And, when understanding dawns here, and victory comes, there will be no greater joy on earth than the joy that fills the hearts of those who experience in this realm the liberating power of the Saviour.

Other titles
by
James Philip
published
by
Christian Focus Publications

(1)The Growing Christian

A very helpful book for Christians with a genuine desire to grow.

(2)The Christian Warfare And Armour

A practical book dealing with Ephesians 6 and the divine provision we have to resist the devil' attacks.